The Pretenders

The Pretenders

Gifted People Who Have

Difficulty Learning

Barbara P. Guyer, Ed.D.

High Tide Press ‡ 1997

A HIGH TIDE BOOK
Published by High Tide Press Inc.
3650 West 183rd Street, Homewood, Illinois 60430
www.hightidepress.com / toll-free 1-888-487-7377

Editorial coordination: John Patrick Grace, Grace Associates,
Ltd., 945 4th Ave., Ste. 200, Huntington, West Virginia 25701

Library of Congress Catalog Card Number: 96-80002
Guyer, Barbara P., The Pretenders: Gifted people who have
difficulty learning / by Barbara P. Guyer, Ed.D. – 1st ed.

ISBN 1-892696-06-1

Book design by Alex Lubertozzi
Illustrations by John Cartwright and Cliff Elliott

Printed in the United States of America

First Edition

To my husband and best friend,
Kenneth E. Guyer Jr.

I thank him for supporting and
encouraging me in everything
I have ever wanted to do.
I could not have done anything
as well as I did without his help.
Most of all, I thank him for
filling my life with great joy
and an endless love.
I am the most fortunate of women.

Out into the cool of the evening
Strolls the Pretender.
He knows that all his hopes and dreams
begin and end there...
Are you there?
Say a prayer for the Pretender,
Who started out so young and strong
Only to surrender.

—*Jackson Browne*
"The Pretender"

Contents

Illustrations

Following page 88:

Illustrations by John Cartwright and Cliff Elliott

Acknowledgments

WORDS SEEM INADEQUATE to express the gratitude that I feel to the many people who have helped to make this book a reality:

To Mary Louise Trusdell, Richmond, Virginia, who introduced me to the world of dyslexia and who taught me how to make it possible for my students to learn to read and write when all else had failed. I am grateful to her for introducing me to the Orton-Gillingham approach for teaching reading, spelling, and handwriting.

To Alice Koontz, Baltimore, Maryland, from whom I have learned more than any other person. She is a master teacher and has joyfully shared her ideas and teaching techniques with me and others, so that those who live in a non-reading world may become literate.

To Dr. Daryll D. Bauer, my chairman in the Department of Special Education at Marshall University, who has given me the freedom to have my own thoughts and be my own person. His understanding and flexibility have made it possible for me to grow as a professional person.

To my daughter, Jennifer Guyer Heiner, who taught me so much when she was suffering as a teenager with a closed-head injury. Through her struggles, I learned what parents go through when a child is hurting. I learned how crucial it is to support your child and let that child know that you will always love her regardless of what happens. I also learned that I must always be gentle, caring, and compassionate when I meet with parents as a professional person. Finally, I learned that even the "blackest" day can get better.

To my daughter, Greta Guyer Flanagan, who has understood and forgiven me for failing to diagnose her problems with dyslexia and ADD. Her story in this book explains the gratitude I feel and the great love I have for her.

To my mother, who taught me that all people have something loveable within them, although it may be difficult to find. She taught me that thoughts are very important things, and that if one is to succeed, it is essential to think positively. If one wants one's students to read and succeed, it is important to see them as successes rather than as hopeless illiterates.

To my father, George David Priddy Jr., whose battle with alcoholism taught me so many lessons. They were lessons that I resented as a child. But, as an adult, I have found that what I learned from him gave me the insight to help many others who are battling a variety of problems, from alcohol to poor self-esteem.

To the many young people with whom I have worked through the years, I owe you so much. I have certainly learned more from you than I ever could have hoped to teach. How fortunate I am that our paths have crossed!

To those who have helped me with the finishing touches of this book, I am very grateful: Julia Shepherd, Michael Dolin, Patrick Grace, and Alex Lubertozzi.

Foreword

by Sally E. Shaywitz, M.D.

THE STORIES THAT form Barbara Guyer's *The Pretenders* both begin and culminate with a very personal story; as the book begins we learn about Jennifer, the author's younger daughter, who develops learning difficulties following an accident, and in the closing chapter we share Dr. Guyer's anguish as a mother who discovers that her eldest daughter — now a young physician — is both dyslexic and ADHD. It is no accident that the stories of Dr. Guyer's students here are embraced by those relating to her own children and to her own personal experiences with each of her daughters' learning difficulties, for it is the ability to put a warm and personal face on what it means to be learning disabled that is the very unique contribution of this volume. Dr. Guyer writes about a group of individuals, men and women from all walks of life, who share a common element — significant reading difficulties in the face of above average to highly gifted levels of intellect.

The Pretenders comes at a particularly opportune time, a time when the very possibility of a reading disability in highly gifted individuals is often questioned and frequently misunderstood. What Dr. Guyer has accomplished in this simple, graceful, and highly accessible volume is to make the notion of reading disability and its consequences for the individual, for his or her family, for educators and for society, come to life. The reader will be deeply moved, as I was, after meeting and reading about these diverse individuals: Jennifer, who, despite many setbacks goes on to become an attorney who has not lost a case in two years; Richie, a young boy with hyperactivity, whose mother is told that she is to blame for his troubles in school; Craig, a college student whose mother "seemed to be accustomed to fighting for her son," who just wanted to be like everyone else; Andy, also a college student, for whom the recurring message of you are "just too dumb to learn" led to such a sense of sadness that his mother could not remember the last time he smiled; Eric, a medical student with an IQ in the "highly gifted" range, but who loses confidence in himself and is essentially rescued by a "perceptive and well-informed" Dean who "looked beyond lack of ability and laziness as the only possible reasons for academic failure;" Wanda, who is both the wife of a successful businessman and illiterate, is "scarred not only by her illiteracy but also by the thoughtlessness of others from her past...;" Dave, who is intelligent, well-informed, and perceptive, but who is not able to write a letter to a dying friend; Cornelius, a college athlete with an IQ close to the superior range, but who went through his school system labeled as mentally retarded and, perhaps, most poignant of all, Greta, Dr. Guyer's oldest daughter, who is diagnosed with dyslexia and ADHD only after she completes medical school—a diagnosis that causes her mother to feel "like a failure," but brings relief at last to the child.

After reading *The Pretenders* there will be no question of what it means at a very personal level to be very bright and, at the same time, dyslexic, nor will there be any question of the deep wounds suffered by such individuals at the hands of often insensitive and uninformed educators and others. Most important of all, there will be no question of the tremendous potential and ability that lies within such individuals—potential waiting to be released and allowed to be put to use. What an unfortunate world it would be if we were to be denied the sharp legal mind and dedication of a Jennifer Guyer, the talents of a future caring educator like Cornelius, or the rare skill, informed insights, and unusual empathy displayed by physicians such as Eric and Greta. Reading about these intelligent men and women with dyslexia, whose ethos is perseverance and refusal to give up — even in the face of the most frustrating and disheartening of circumstances — we come to better understand why they, and unknown others whom they represent, "deserve a chance to try" and why we as a society are better off if they are allowed to use their talents to pursue their individual dreams and hopes. Dr. Guyer, in relating these stories, skillfully teases apart substance from form, intelligence from facility in reading, knowledge from scores on standardized tests, so that the reader can clearly comprehend why "sometimes the best students don't make the best lawyers [doctors, teacher, etc.]; instead sometimes those who haven't done as well in the classroom make excellent lawyers [doctors, teachers, etc.]."

Each of the stories told by Dr. Guyer is compelling and has a powerful impact that cannot be ignored; I was deeply moved by these stories. As a physician-scientist whose own clinical experience caring for dyslexic children and then adults served as the impetus for my research into the basic neurobiology underlying dyslexia, I was especially drawn to the stories of Eric and, of course, Greta. It is often such particularly bright and sensitive individuals as Eric and Greta who bear the full brunt of misinformed, stereotyped views of dyslexia. There is so much to be learned from their life experiences, the quiet, and often unnoticed small humiliations, the tendency for educators and school counselors to focus on weaknesses and to be blinded to significant strengths. As Barbara Guyer so aptly put it, "It saddened me that in all of our conferences, none of her first teachers mentioned Greta's above average intelligence. They only mentioned her weaknesses." The shame experienced in the classroom over and over again exacts a toll, and it comes as no surprise that Eric believes he is mentally retarded until he is brought to Dr. Guyer's attention by his Dean, tested, and found to have an IQ in the highly gifted range. One can only imagine all of the Erics who do not have such insightful Deans and whose great gifts go unrecognized, unrewarded, and lost to themselves and to society. Greta, too, thinks she is mentally retarded until she is tested in junior high school and found to qualify for the Gifted and Talented Program.

Both Eric and Greta endure childhoods characterized by hard work with little time for play, but both grow up to be extremely compassionate, sensitive, and intelligent adults whose life stories serve as definitions of character and resiliency. What makes it possible for the Erics and Gretas of the world to succeed? Unusual intelligence, incredible motivation and perseverance, and the support of adults who believe in them—their parents and teachers, and, in Eric's life, the Dean of his medical school. Eric and Greta are not exceptions, as part of my work at the National Institute of Child Health and Human Development—Yale Center for the Study of Learning and Attention, I have encountered many other dyslexic medical students, scientists, and faculty who are among the most creative and talented individuals in medicine. They, too, share the same life histories, feelings of shame and humiliation, superior intelligence, extraordinary devotion, and empathy for their patients. It saddens me when I see gifted medical students judged not by their clinical acumen, insights, and compassion, but instead by scores on a standardized test whose relationship to being a good doctor has yet to be demonstrated.

I believe it is terribly important for these stories to be told and the lessons from them to be taken seriously. As a physician, I can speak authoritatively on the importance of including individuals like Eric and Greta within the medical fraternity, for these are precisely the kinds of physicians that medicine now needs. They are the people who offer hope for the future of medicine. As Eric was told on gaining acceptance to a highly competitive residency in reconstructive surgery:

> We selected you because you're unique. Straight A medical graduates aren't that hard to find. We've learned that straight A students don't always make the best physicians. On the other hand, you've had a problem, but you have worked to overcome it with everything

that's in you. You could have given up but you didn't... I know some professors said you would never make it, but you didn't quit. You're persistent, Eric. And that's why we selected you. You're a survivor. We believe you're the type of person who will make an exceptionally good reconstructive surgeon.

Eric successfully completed his surgical residency and is on his way to becoming an "outstanding surgeon who publishes papers in medical journals and presents papers at medical conferences." As Dr. Guyer puts it, "How different Eric's life could have been. He might have attended a medical school which simply dismissed students not maintaining the required grade point average. Fortunately for Eric and probably for all of us, someone wanted to find out why a student was failing. Because of a highly professional and observant Dean, Eric will not be a frustrated and hurt young man in search of a profession outside of medicine."

Medicine is in need of individuals like Eric and Greta who are not so perfect that they cannot relate to and have a sense of shared experience with their patients. I have seen too many medical students, and indeed, physicians who, never having experienced any significant adversity, find it hard to relate to the difficulties described by their patients—a stroke patient now having difficulty speaking, an elderly man who must be in a wheelchair, or a patient with congestive heart failure who can no longer climb steps. Most of the practice of medicine is not made up of those acute, dramatic moments shown on television shows, but is rather comprised of diagnosing and then supporting patients through rather undramatic, but often doggedly persistent chronic illnesses that quietly erode away at the patient's (and his or her loved ones) energies and sense of self. Their own life experiences have provided dyslexic doctors with a very special and unique perspective: even at a relatively young age they know what it is like to suffer, to fail and yet not to give up. Where fellow medical students of the same age may be brash and impatient, dyslexic medical students and doctors already have learned that living life is a marathon and not a sprint.

They know what it is to live with a disability and, as a result, bring to the care of their patients a sensitivity and understanding that no course in medical school can ever possibly instill. Just as Dr. Guyer has noted, time and time again, patients and preceptors alike have commented on the extraordinary patience, empathy, willingness and ability to communicate with patients and their families demonstrated by individual students and physicians who I know are dyslexic. As many of us have learned, mistakes made by doctors rarely arise out of lack of knowledge; they reflect more often a lack of commitment to their patients, a failure to care and, particularly, to listen and to take seriously the complaints of their patients. The intelligence, devotion, and compassion shown by dyslexic physicians indicate that they are just the ones who will provide their patients with the highest quality of care.

We, as physicians and as a society in general, have acknowledged the great need for diversity within the community of physicians. Just as it has been important historically to open the circle of physicians to include individuals representing all religions, races, and both sexes, it is now time to allow other capable groups to be incorporated into the tapestry of medicine—including individuals who are bright, compassionate, and also dyslexic. Dyslexic medical students have much to teach their fellow students and future physicians about chronic disability, adversity, and resilience, and much to contribute to the care and well-being of their future patients.

The Pretenders will help to ensure that these deserving individuals are given the opportunity they so richly deserve and that medicine and patients will have the opportunity to benefit from their contributions. *The Pretenders* should be read not only by all medical school Deans, but by faculty everywhere and by dyslexic students themselves.

Yale University
School of Medicine

Preface

A FEW YEARS AGO I assigned the anecdotal book, *Turnabout Children* by Mary MacCracken, for my "Introduction to Learning Disabilities" course. The book gathered stories of eight children with whom Ms. MacCracken had worked professionally. One of my graduate students later told me, "I really enjoyed that book, but I wish the author had let us know what happens to such special people when they become adults."

The book you hold in your hands is a response to that student's wish. The people whose stories I recount here are people with whom I have worked professionally over the years. They have all overcome incredible obstacles to achieve success in their fields and in their home lives—in part because their vocabularies do not include the words, "I can't." While these sturdy souls are in the act of falling, they are already planning how to pick themselves up and fight back to the top.

Richie, who grew up with my children, somehow managed to survive a childhood of what some might have termed "just impossible" hyperactivity—a whirling dervish. With his perpetual motion act and his bedeviling antics, I'm sure that Richie gave many of his regular classroom teachers premature gray hair. Anyone who knew Richie could never blot him out of memory. You prayed that he would not come into your yard, because he would never leave it in the same state in which he found it. What caused the metamorphosis in Richie's life that allowed him to develop a successful carpentry business? For one thing, he made a good choice in a marriage partner. His wife of fifteen years can take a certain amount of credit for his turnaround. She never let Richie's whirlwind ways destroy her positive concept of him and their relationship; and she was always ready with her unflagging encouragement to help him past the rough places. To see Richie today, with a full and happy family and work life, you would never guess how bleak his future looked to those who knew him as a teenager.

Wanda is beautiful, inside and out. Her fresh approach to life warms every heart around her. Amazingly, she grew to adulthood and married a well-educated man, all the while pretending to do something she couldn't—read. Her problem was dyslexia, which she battles to this day. Thanks to counseling and a very loving and understanding family, however, Wanda no longer cares who learns about a problem that she kept secret for years. Now she fends off embarrassment with a smile and a tremendous sense of humor.

And then there's Eric, a man with a genius IQ who carried an A average through high school and college, yet almost got dropped from medical school in his first year. Eric was my introduction to a segment of our population that I never even thought existed— truly gifted people who never experience failure until they reach a level where they can no longer compensate for a developmental flaw.

Eric's story, like those of others profiled here, has a happy ending. Seeing Eric successful and fulfilled and knowing that I had a small part to play in his positive changes has been one of my life's great rewards.

One story in this book was particularly difficult for me to write—the story of my own daughter, Greta. Though I was trained to diagnose the learning disabilities that weighed on her, and had done so with numerous others who came to me for help, I missed diagnosing her problems completely. It fell to another professional, very late in Greta's education, to bring reality home to me.

"Barbara," this colleague said, "your daughter tests positive not only for dyslexia, but also for attention deficit disorder [ADD]." This was a very anguishing and humbling experience, one that still pains me as I share it.

My hope for you, the readers of this book, is that the stories of the unforgettable people recounted here will help you to understand similar problems in your own life or in the life of someone who is important to you — a spouse, a child, a student, a colleague, or a friend.

Having reading problems is different from any other problem a person might be challenged with. If you can't draw or sing or play a musical instrument, if you can't balance a checkbook, or if you fail in an attempt to master a computer program, or the elements of biology, you can probably laugh about it. But if you can't read words on paper, you will typically feel ashamed and try to hide this gap from everyone you meet. Each time you tell a lie to mask your problem, your self-esteem goes down another notch. I know that's what happens to people with learning disabilities because I've seen it over and over.

May the people in this book, these wonderful, plucky spirits, provide hope to all who are intelligent but have trouble with reading — and even give them the courage to disclose their problems to those whom they love and trust.

Marshall University
Huntington, West Virginia
October 1996

The Pretenders

chapter 1

initiation

THE PERSONNEL DIRECTOR of a large public school system looked at me intently over his half-glasses. "Mrs. Guyer, would you be interested in teaching a learning disabilities class? I notice that you have a good reading background." I had the feeling he was trying to decide just how far I would go to get a job. The director looked at me expectantly and added, "This is a self-contained class." He waited for some response from me.

I wasn't sure just what learning disabilities were. My mind raced, searching for a memory of the term. What was different about children who have so much trouble learning that they have to be placed in a separate class?

"Sure. I'll be glad to give it a try. You understand that I really don't have a background in learning disabilities, but I work hard and learn quickly," I reassured the man. He looked relieved. After all, it was only two weeks before school started and that class still didn't have a teacher. I wasn't wise enough to ask how many teachers had taught the class in the past, or ask about the kinds of learning disabilities these children had. I should have. I had no idea what was in store for me or I wouldn't have slept during the two weeks before school began. I just thought of some sweet little children who couldn't read, and I was going to be the person who changed their lives. They would be so grateful to me. It would be the most rewarding year of teaching I had ever had. Dream on!

During the two weeks I read several very boring books on

learning disabilities. Much more interesting were my two active young daughters who constantly demanded my attention by getting into things they shouldn't be in. Nevertheless, I managed to brush up on my skills in reading, spelling, and arithmetic. I felt ready to teach when the first day of school began. My husband and I planned out the routine: he takes our daughters to the local Montessori school, my retired father picks them up after school, and I get the girls at my father's home when my school is over. We seemed to have everything worked out perfectly for me to return to teaching after five years off to be at home with our children.

The first day of school I arrived early so I could have everything in order for my students. There would be twelve of them, riding various buses, but all arriving within thirty minutes after school began. All the better. I would have everything in perfect order. This was going to be the year these kids learned something.

I was working at my desk, enjoying the peaceful surroundings, when the quiet erupted into loud noises. "You dirty, rotten *&%@#*. You leave me alone or I'll break every rotten bone in your rotten body!" Two large boys, both dirty, around thirteen years of age, burst into my room. They looked me over suspiciously, never smiling or saying hello.

"Good morning, boys. I'm Mrs. Guyer, your new teacher." I decided to ignore the yelling in the hall and try to get off on the right foot.

One boy pushed the other and they both started to giggle. Soon they were laughing uncontrollably. One boy fell on the floor and literally rolled around while he laughed. I wasn't sure what to do next. This was a new type of experience for me. I didn't yet know it was only the first of many new experiences to follow.

The door to the classroom opened again and a boy with large blue eyes entered, accompanied by his mother. She immediately impressed me as a person I liked. Her warm smile and ready handshake relieved the rather bizarre meeting I had just had with the two boys.

"This is Tom," the mother said. "I'm Charlotte Adkins. You probably know from his records that Tom is autistic."

I attempted to smile knowingly. What records? I had received no records on any of the students. "They are on the way," a secretary at the downtown office had assured me when I called about records a week before.

So far my LD class had two boys who looked like juvenile delinquents and one autistic boy. What next?

The classroom door opened a third time and the other nine students entered together because they had all come on the same bus. One little boy who reminded me of a plucked chicken did cartwheels across the classroom. Between each one he looked quickly at me to make sure I was watching. Oh, I was watching all right. My eyes nearly popped out of my head.

Tom's mother gave a run down on all of the children. She became my *de facto* substitute for school records, and she had no idea just how much I appreciated her inside information.

"The monkey who just flew in is Bobby. He's schizophrenic and very hyperactive. You'll have to let him know you're running things today or he'll take over." I smiled faintly, wondering why on earth I was in that room. What had I done to merit this punishment?

At that moment another student entered the room. He had red, curly hair with prominent freckles on his face. His bright blue eyes captured my attention right away. He smiled somewhat sadly as he took a seat. Charlotte softly muttered, "John Anderson is a boy who will worm his way into your heart right away. He's so lovable, but at the same time he can be exasperating."

"What do you mean?" I asked.

"Shh, he's watching. I'll tell you another time. You'll soon find out for yourself anyway."

Charlotte quietly described the other children in the class. She could be only so quiet, however, because the two dirty boys (John and Albert, I learned) were now fighting, Bobby was standing on one of the study carrels, and Tom was trying to sit in my lap. Although Tom was tall for his ten years, his favorite activity was to lie in someone's lap in a fetal position. Charlotte took Tom's hand and led him to his seat. She handed him a book and he began to read.

I didn't want Charlotte to leave. I had never been afraid of a group of children before, but I had never been exposed to a group like this one. Before she left, Charlotte gave me the lowdown on Billy, who had severe dyslexia. He couldn't read a word, and his anger about being a nonreader made him hostile to everyone, especially teachers. Billy was from a large family who had come here from South America shortly before he was born. Billy had been an enigma to all of his teachers because he remained a non-reader in spite of concerted efforts on their part. His behavior became worse as he got older.

Marilyn was a quiet, polite ten-year-old girl for whom I was very thankful. How could I protect her from her wild classmates? Then there was Raymond, whose deep blue eyes and shy smile made him very appealing. He couldn't read anything either. In fact, I later learned that Tom, Charlotte's autistic son, was the only student in my class who could read. Tom read anything and everything. He especially loved reading the encyclopedia. He would begin with a letter in the morning and complete it in a day or so. Tom usually rocked as he read, laughing aloud when something amused him. The other children often laughed at him, but I could tell they envied him because he could read. Most of the children carried books when they went home, trying to pretend they could read them.

Charlotte mentioned again that she had to leave. She worked all night as a nurse at a local hospital and needed some sleep. A single parent, she worked the night shift in order to be with her son during the afternoon and evening. She rarely worked on weekends so that she and Tom could go on short trips. Tom kept one notebook for road signs and another for menus. After he left a restaurant he always reproduced the menu in his notebook. Charlotte said he made few errors.

Charlotte left me to face this group of wild people by myself. I told them my name and about my family. I asked them their names. They were well-behaved then, and we discussed what they liked about school and what they didn't like. All they liked about school was recess, lunch, and leaving. We talked about how I was going to try to help them learn what they needed to know to be good students. They looked at me as if they didn't believe me. I suppose when you've failed as often as they had, it's difficult to believe any teacher who says she is going to change your life.

It didn't take long for me to realize that none of my students could read at all with the one exception of the autistic boy, who read anything and everything indiscriminately. An encyclopedia entertained him for hours. My immediate job was to teach these children to read and write. I tried every technique I had ever been taught in undergraduate and graduate classes. I carefully searched through all my textbooks in vain. There seemed to be nothing in my books or notes that helped. Most of the techniques I had been taught involved a variety of whole word approaches or the "look-say" method. By Christmas my students had learned almost nothing that they remembered a week later, and their behavior had become intolerable. I was in contention for the title of The World's Most Frustrated Teacher.

Then there was John. Charlotte was right. I will never forget him as long as I live. As soon as he sat down the first day, he reached into his pocket and pulled out Gumby and Pokey and began talking to them nonstop. (He talked for Gumby and Pokey.) About a week later I had had all I could take of those three. I walked over to John's desk and snatched Gumby and Pokey from his hands. "They need a rest, John," I said. "I'll take good care of them until it's time for you to go home. See? I'm putting them in my desk drawer. They aren't far away." I smiled to myself, thinking I had paved the way for a quiet afternoon. With that, however, John began to scream, "You're suffocating them! Help! Help! You're killing them!"

I stood my ground. "No, John, I am opening the drawer so they can breathe. See? They're fine." John did his work for a minute or two. Then he came to my desk to get a Kleenex. He returned to his seat and worked on the tissue. In less than a minute he was engaged in deep conversation with Casper the Friendly Ghost.

Two weeks later John developed a new love. He brought an imaginary motorcycle to school. This wouldn't have been so bad, except that he kept revving the engine all day. Once, when I was ready to scream, I walked to John's desk, took the key out of his "motorcycle," and said, "There, John. I've got the key. Now you can't drive it any more until after school. I'll return the key then." John sat for a moment. I thought I had put one over on him, but then he smiled broadly and revved the motor. "John," I said, "you can't do that. I have the key to your motorcycle!"

"I had another key," he said and smiled as he revved the engine again. I put my head down on my desk in utter defeat.

Two of my students left me for one blessed hour each day to be tutored by a person the children called "the dyslexia lady." I could see that only these two students were learning reading and spelling skills. After one particularly bad day I went to Mrs. True's room in tears and explained that I couldn't seem to teach the other students anything they remembered the next day. I wiped my eyes and asked, "Can you help me? The only students I have who are learning anything are your students too."

Mrs. True, a kind and generous lady, is probably the best teacher I've ever known. She has that rare gift every teacher should have but few actually possess. She smiled and said, "I know you've tried your best, Barbara, but the techniques you've been using usually don't work with students who reverse and transpose letters as often as your students do. Why don't I come to your class for an hour each day during the students' private tutoring time. Maybe I can give you some pointers." I quickly agreed. This would give me an opportunity to observe her teaching and learn on the job.

The next day was an unforgettable joy for me. I watched as this gifted teacher worked with each child, assessing problems and strengths. She soon discovered they didn't understand letter/sound correspondence (the relationship between the letter and the sound that goes with it), so she began teaching that with a number of basic letters. During the next week she gradually introduced nine letters that were not similar. For example, she introduced *b* but not *d*, and *p* but not *g*. Then she attached a concrete object to each letter by always having a picture of an object that began with that letter sound. If the students couldn't remember the sound of the letter, they could remember the object that began with that sound (*b*/boy, for example). The students would look at the letter on a card and then say the name of the letter, the clue word (boy), the sound of the letter, and the name of the letter again. Then they wrote the letter. This technique helped to bridge the gap between the abstract letters of the alphabet and the concrete lives of the children.

We went over these letters every day, eliminating the letters they knew and adding new letters or combinations (*sh, wh*). Then Mrs. True helped the students blend the sounds into words. I thought this would never happen, but it did. She put a picture above each letter of the word they were to read. The students would try to say the sounds of the word. If they forgot, they could look at the objects above the letters which gave them trouble and say the sounds.

One boy in the class, the most severe dyslexic I have known, used this as an aid for one year; then he began to read rather fluently, apparently having bridged the gap between illiteracy and literacy. I was tempted to use the word "crutch" instead of "aid," but so many people have negative feelings about the crutches people use. A psychologist whom I respect very much once asked me, "Do you know anyone who uses a crutch after his broken leg has healed?" I confessed that I did not. "Then don't expect people to use a crutch in reading when they don't need it." That made a lot of sense to me, and I have felt differently about crutches or aids ever since. I wish he could have talked with the many teachers who refuse to let children count on their fingers. What's wrong with that? Surely they wouldn't count this way if it weren't necessary, and they will put away the crutch when it's no longer needed.

Gradually Mrs. True taught the children syllable division rules, which made it possible for them to read longer words that had short vowels, such as *fan/tas/tic*. She also taught them spelling rules by using discovery teaching and a multi-sensory approach. Mrs. True believed one should teach reading, spelling, and handwriting together. She explained to me that these children needed to be over-taught. Therefore, she had them read what they were learning to spell, spell the words they were reading, and practice their handwriting using the same letters and words. This seemed a wise approach to use with all children. I've always wondered why we have separate, unrelated books for reading, spelling, and handwriting.

Mrs. True continued seeing my students daily, and I was learning how to use her teaching techniques. My class was riding high. Anyone could see they were beginning to feel that they might learn to read after all. Maybe life wouldn't be so unbearable as they once thought. I watched with an inexpressible joy as the children began to read small books. *Fat Sam* was the first book they read. One thirteen-year-old boy brought his book up to my desk with tears in his eyes.

"This is the first book I've ever read and really know what I'm reading. I've read pictures before, but this time I read real words!" I'll never forget the expression on his face. That is what makes teaching a profession I will never leave, regardless of the salary.

Each child began to change slowly. Bobby, the hyperactive plucked chicken, actually walked into our classroom most of the time. Albert, the juvenile delinquent, didn't fight at every opportunity, and occasionally I even saw his beautiful smile. His entire face lit up when he smiled. Billy, the South American boy, probably changed more than anyone in the class. He made more progress than some of the other students, probably because he saw Mrs. True once a day individually in addition to the hour she spent with the class as a whole. He began to chat with me amicably during the school day instead of glaring at me. He confided in me several times, and I felt so privileged that he felt he could trust me.

One day Billy came to class very upset. His face was dirty and his cheeks were covered with tears. I had never seen him this way before. Usually he tried to be very macho. I took Billy's hand and we walked to the back of the room where there was a coat closet. This would give us a limited amount of privacy. I stooped down so I would be closer to him and asked, "What's wrong, Billy? Please tell me so I can try to help." He looked at me intently, trying to decide if he should trust me. Evidently he decided he could and spoke in a low tone of voice to be sure I was the only one who could hear.

"My big brother, James, was arrested last night. He's in jail right now. My mother doesn't have any money to get him out. She doesn't want anybody to know he's in jail. Promise you won't tell."

"I won't tell anyone if you don't want me to," I reassured Billy. "Tell me, son, why was he arrested? What did the police say he did?"

"The police said he stole a car. He really did, but you know why? He was going to surprise our mother with some groceries. He was going to take me with him to the store. We already made out the list the other day. With what was left over we were going to buy her a new dress. He promised me it wouldn't get him in any trouble. See, this guy wanted James to ride around with him and look for a car that brings a good price. When they found the right car, James was supposed to hot wire it and take it to an address the guy wrote down."

I could visualize Billy's brother, desperate for money, being taken advantage of by a neighborhood thug. The fellow who had planned everything was long gone when the police came, of course. Somehow I had to convince Billy to let me try to help him and his family. Finally he agreed that his mother could be called. At that moment I was very grateful we had a social worker assigned to our school.

Mr. Adams, the social worker, was in the building. I sent for him to come to my classroom. After some persuasion, Billy told him everything he had told me. The three of us agreed that Mr. Adams could go to see Billy's mother in an effort to resolve the problem with the incarcerated brother. When Mr. Adams went to the home, he was able to talk with Billy's mother easily because he understood Spanish. It seemed that Billy was telling the truth. This was James' first arrest, and the purpose of the theft apparently was for buying food for the family. The grocery list was in his pocket along with Mrs. Day's dress size. Since this was James' first offense, he was released in the care of his mother.

Mrs. Day also told Mr. Adams about another family problem. It seems that the boys' father was not dead. In fact, he was very much alive. He had come to the family's modest apartment two months ago, saying he was going to take care of them all. Each day, however, he postponed looking for a job by making various excuses, such as illness or prejudice by employers against South Americans. He drained the family's resources and soon there was nothing left. To satisfy his extensive need for alcohol, he forcefully took money the family needed for food to make his personal purchases at the liquor store. When drinking, he was impossible to be with. He hit Mrs. Day many times. When he started beating the boys, she tried to defend them, which usually resulted in a free-for-all with much screaming and cursing. On one particularly violent night, Mr. Day attacked his wife in front of the boys, ripping off her dress and under garments. He then raped her while the two boys gaped in silence, tears streaming down their faces. Their father had a large knife which he threatened to use on their mother if the boys so much as moved. Mrs. Day wept quietly for most of the night, and Billy and James took turns trying to comfort her. She was bruised and had several cuts. Mr. Day left after the attack and went to one of the local bars, taking with him the grocery money. No wonder Billy had difficulty concentrating in school. I had no idea he had witnessed such behavior, or that his father wasn't really dead.

A few nights after the boys' father had attacked their mother, Mr. Day was particularly pleasant while they had dinner together as a family. The dinner left much to be desired, and they were all still hungry when everything had been eaten. Mr. Day said he needed to go to the store and invited Billy to accompany him, promising that he would buy him a popsicle. Overwhelmed with joy, Billy was ready to go in an instant. His father had never paid so much attention to him before.

Billy and his father did not go to the grocery store. Instead, they went to a bar about ten blocks from the apartment. Mr. Day sat at a round table with five or six disreputable, dirty men. He made Billy sit on his lap and began drinking. As he became intoxicated, he bragged about his sexual abilities and how his children had inherited all of his skills. He said Billy was by far the best and would be available to the highest bidder for the night. The men looked at Billy and touched him and pulled at his clothing, trying to decide if Mr. Day was lying. Finally, to Billy's utter horror, they began bidding. One ugly, dirty man offered $10; another offered $15. The last man said he would pay $20. The frightened boy tried to run, but his father grabbed his hand, taking the $20 with his other hand. The man agreed to return Billy to the bar the next evening.

When Mr. Day returned home without Billy, his wife was frantic. He assured her that he was spending the night with a nice family and would be back the next afternoon. He convinced Mrs. Day that Billy was safe, so she patiently waited for the next day when Billy would be home.

The next afternoon Billy returned home, his clothes torn, his body bruised and scratched. He had escaped from the evil man who "rented" him for the night, but only after the man had raped him repeatedly. He tied Billy to the bed so he couldn't get away and put a dirty rag in his mouth so the neighbors wouldn't hear him screaming and pleading. The boy had never experienced anything like this, and he returned home in a state of shock. He didn't want to upset his mother by telling her the gory details, but he couldn't seem to help himself. Bit by bit the story came out, interrupted by sobs and violent shaking. Mrs. Day, from fear of her husband, did nothing, until the social worker went to her home. His ability to speak Spanish made it easier for her to confide in him. As she talked, Mr. Adams vowed he would help this troubled, desperate family.

It took some time, but we were able to get a restraining order keeping Mr. Day from the home. There were no charges against him made by Mrs. Day because she didn't want him to be vindictive. She felt confident her children would be safe with the restraining order. Mr. Adams was able to obtain an increase in the amount of money that Mrs. Day received. The amount was small, but it helped. He also found a job for her as a housekeeper with a Mexican family who had recently moved to town. Mrs. Day and her two sons could live in a lovely garage apartment on the property of the Mexican family. It was beginning to look as if the quality of life was improving for the Day family.

Billy continued in my class after his family moved. I was very grateful for that because I felt too many changes in his life at one time would be difficult for him. Besides, he was making good progress in reading and spelling for the first time in his life. It would not be wise to disrupt such a miracle.

Unfortunately, not every student made lasting progress. The last time I saw John he was walking down the street, deep in conversation with Gumby and Pokey, who were in his shirt pocket. They were his best friends, his only friends, except for Casper the Ghost.

I managed to survive the year with my first LD class, thanks to Mrs. True, and I'm sure I learned more than my students. Several of them came to my home during the summer months so I could keep them from forgetting what had been learned during the school year. Some of my friends tutored for a fee during the summer, but I worked with these unique young people for nothing more than the smile I received when they were successful. Some of them could have paid but most could not, and it was easier to charge no one. Working individually with students was much easier than working in small groups, and they learned so much more quickly. In a group situation many students are embarrassed when they make mistakes. Whereas, in an individual setting, this isn't a problem. They had learned to trust me and weren't embarrassed when they made errors in my presence.

Since that time I have met countless people who couldn't read: black and white, tall and short, fat and thin, brilliant and below average, pretty and ugly, well-adjusted or deeply scarred by their reading failure. They were all so different that I began to understand why learning disabilities are such a controversial area. Some could read but couldn't spell, some could spell but couldn't read, and some couldn't make an *s* that anyone could read. A few students could remember everything they heard but couldn't read a textbook. Some had almost no attention span, and some (like the plucked chicken in my first LD class) were so hyperactive they couldn't learn. They are certainly different.

☼ ☼ ☼

When my younger daughter Jennifer was sixteen years old, I learned personally what it means to have a child who has a learning disability. She had always been particularly gifted in all areas of language, and in the fifth grade she was testing on a college level on achievement tests. She and her sister attended a Montessori school. My husband and I felt that the multi-sensory approach to education had contributed significantly toward making them skilled in reading and written language.

When Jennifer was sixteen years of age she went on a canoeing trip for one week through a church camp. When my daughter's canoe approached a waterfall, she was knocked out of the canoe after bumping into a partially submerged rock. Jennifer was unconscious for a few minutes, and someone rescued her at the bottom of the waterfall. She was taken to a nearby doctor who felt that she was not injured.

After returning home from the canoe trip, our family went on a two-week vacation. During this time Jennifer and her sister spent much of their time swimming and water-skiing. I noticed that Jennifer did not read at all, which was unusual for her. When school began in the fall, she began bringing failing grades home. Since she was in the gifted program, grades that were in the twenty-five to fifty range were previously unheard of. One afternoon Jennifer mentioned that she couldn't copy from the board and said she thought she needed to have her eyes examined. The specialist we usually use could not see her for six months, so I made an appointment with a new person in town. When Jennifer went for the eye examination, I went with her. I was amazed when, halfway through the exam, she began to jerk violently and lost consciousness. This appeared to me to be a *grand mal* seizure. Jennifer slept all the way home and for the rest of the evening. She seemed disoriented and told me that the corners of rooms appeared to be rounded. She also said that she heard music when there wasn't any. I knew that these are all symptomatic of a seizure disorder, and I called our pediatrician. She suggested that Jennifer see a neurologist and have an EEG (electroencephalogram), a test to measure brain waves. I sat with the neurologist as she examined Jennifer's EEG.

"What has happened to Jennifer lately?" she asked. I didn't know of anything. When Jennifer had completed the test, the neurologist repeated her question. "I fell down a waterfall last summer and was unconscious for a few minutes," Jennifer responded. This was the first I heard of the accident. No one at the camp told us about it, and Jennifer didn't mention it because she wanted to be able to return the next summer! The neurologist put my daughter on medication to control seizure disorder, and this did seem to help. Her problems with organization, word retrieval, memory, reading, and written language continued to be a serious problem, however.

In trying to find an answer, my husband and I took Jennifer to three major medical centers. The University of Virginia seemed to help us the most because of the neuro-psychological testing that indicated that Jennifer had a bruised brain. The neuro-psychologist stated that he felt her symptoms would change as the bruise changed. Jennifer dropped out of the gifted program and enrolled in some basic classes where she felt more comfortable. The regular psychological counseling probably saved her life—and ours. The depression which accompanied the vast changes in our daughter's life was sometimes overwhelming. Many evenings she locked herself in her room and refused to open the door or respond when we asked if she was all right. On several of these occasions I prayed for guidance. Each time I did our doorbell rang during the course of the evening. It was one of Jennifer's classmates who had been concerned about her and had brought her a milk shake or an ice cream cone to "cheer her up." One girl who will always be especially dear to me walked three miles in bitter cold to bring Jennifer a milk shake after school. She was concerned when Jennifer was absent from school and came to let her know she missed her. I felt particularly guilty in not being able to give her a ride home. My car was being repaired, and my husband was attending a dinner meeting. I have thought of that experience often and wished that I had thought to pay for a taxi for this exceptional teenager. I have wondered what became of her. She seemed to be very wise for her years.

Jennifer graduated from high school with a C average and said she wanted to major in Psychology in college. Her father and I weren't overly confident that she could succeed in college, and we felt strongly that she shouldn't go away to school for the first year. So she reluctantly (even bitterly) agreed to attend Marshall University for her first year. She transferred to a college in another state the following year. She survived many problems with poor grades, depression, and reading and graduated with a C grade-point average and a degree in psychology.

After graduating from college, Jennifer worked in a law office as a "gopher," running errands and so forth. Ever since she was a small child, she wanted to be an attorney, and she mentioned to her father and me that she was very sincere about wanting to go to law school. I urged her to consider something else. She continued to have problems memorizing a great deal of information at one time, and I knew that law school would require extensive memory skills. I'll never forget Jennifer's reaction to what I said. "Mom, you may be right," she said, "but don't you think I deserve a chance to try?" I couldn't argue with that. In fact, I had never won an argument with our youngest daughter since she was six years old. I somehow knew that if she could just get through school, she would be an excellent attorney.

Jennifer attended a small, private law school. She seemed to do well at first, but her grades at the end of the first year were far from encouraging. She was dismissed from the school. At this point, one of her professors approached her. "Jennifer, sometimes the best students don't make the best lawyers; instead, sometimes those who haven't done as well in the classroom make excellent lawyers. In my opinion, you are in this latter group. When you write your appeal to be re-admitted, I would like to speak on your behalf if you are willing." A few weeks later she was re-admitted, in no small part due to the efforts of her understanding professor. Jennifer began the year with renewed determination and energy. She worked tirelessly, often turning down social invitations so that she could study. She had attended the Psychology Clinic at Marshall University to learn techniques to improve her memory so that retrieval would be less difficult for her. The techniques she learned seemed to help.

When Jennifer graduated from law school, our family had quite a celebration, but it was short-lived. She did not pass the bar examination. When the letter arrived, stating that she had failed, Jennifer was devastated. She soon bounced back, however, and she began studying again in earnest. This time she passed the examination with an excellent score. Since that time our daughter, who does not know how to give up, is working for a rather large law firm where she specializes in the practice of discrimination and employment law. In two years of practice, she has not yet lost a case. She is the editor of a newsletter for an organization of women attorneys, and she is active in the American Bar Association. I understand that she is highly respected by her colleagues.

Occasionally, when a college student comes to my office to tell me she is giving up, I tell her about my daughter. It would have been so easy for her to admit defeat on many occasions; however, she never did. A failure seemed to make her more determined than ever that she would reach her goal. Usually when I tell Jennifer's story to depressed college students, I see a new look of hope in their eyes. Jennifer's experience has certainly helped to make me more understanding of other young people who have learning problems. I can also understand how their parents feel in similar situations. Jennifer's experiences have helped to improve the quality of life for many of my students.

✶   ✶   ✶

Our society places so much importance on reading that it has virtually assured many people with serious reading problems of having emotional problems as well. We equate reading with intelligence. The smart kids are in the bluebird reading group. You know the buzzard group even if the groups have no names. Children learn quickly who is on top. We have all had brief encounters with failure and vividly remember how much we hurt.

Sometimes we ached to the very core of our beings. But we could study hard and do much better the next time. What would have happened to us if we couldn't improve? Would we have given up? Would we have tried to hide the fact that we couldn't read? Become behavior problems? Become show-offs? Or would we have continued to fight, never giving up?

This book is about dyslexics who never gave up. The going was extremely rough at times, but they persevered. You will see how they dealt with failure, rejection, ridicule, and, ultimately, success.

chapter 2

richie

WHEN RICHIE WAS four years old, his mother brought him and his younger sister over to our house to play with our two daughters. A handsome, blue-eyed blond, Richie had the look of an angel; but looks deceive—within five minutes I knew this was no ordinary kid. He had the energy of ten boys and the ability to deflect suspicion from his mischief-making until it was too late to stop him.

His hyperactivity, however, was apparent to all. Most of our neighbors felt sorry for Richie's parents and especially for his mother, Alice, who had to take the equivalent of a ride on a bucking bronco just to get her son through each day. Richie never took naps, raced from one thing to another all day long, then struggled through many restless nights in search of sleep.

This incredible bundle of energy constituted one never-ending series of accidents just waiting to happen.

Probably what got Richie into more trouble than anything else was that he appeared to act first, and think about his actions only later.

One day I glanced out our living room window and spied Richie, who was then age nine, walking toward our cul-de-sac. I whispered a prayer that he would choose not to stop at our yard. God must have been asleep at the switch, for up walked Richie. We had just gotten a swimming pool for our two daughters, and two of their inflated-plastic swans were at that moment turning lazy circles on the water. Quietly swinging the gate of our chain-link fence, Richie entered the yard. I didn't follow him closely with my eyes, but I gathered that he had strolled quickly through our yard and had left by the back gate.

I heaved a sigh of relief.

It was shortly afterward, while taking a bag out to the trash can, that I looked into the pool and saw the two toy swans still floating about, but minus their heads. Richie, in a twinkling, had decapitated them

This little piece of vandalism occurred just one day after he had taken clothes from a little boy across the street and flung them up into a tree.

Richie's parents? Fine people, both of them, so fine it was hard to be angry with them over their turbulent son's shenanigans. Everyone knew they were doing their best to rein him in. After I cooled off from the demise of our toy swans, I decided not to even call them about it. But the next time I saw Richie I asked him, "Weren't you the one who cut the heads off the swans in our pool?" He hung his head and looked as if he wanted to be swallowed up by the earth.

"Why did you do it, Richie?" I asked, my tone softening.

"I don't know," he said, and hung his head even lower.

I couldn't help but feel sorry for him.

I didn't know what else to do but implore him to be more careful in the future and avoid doing impulsive things. Forgiven, he flashed his winsome smile and rushed off—to somebody else's yard.

One afternoon I was a spectator at a boys' softball game. Richie was among the players. The other boys valued his playing skills, and this he seemed to need for his self-concept. However, at one point, Richie thought it was his turn to bat when the smallest boy on his team stepped to the plate instead. Rather than call out, "Hey, I'm up next, not you," Richie ran over and knocked the boy flat on his back. Then he stepped up to home plate, ready to take his swings. The umpire threw him out of the game. He left, I thought, without really understanding what he had done that was so wrong.

A week later Richie, his sister, and my daughter were all playing together. Richie's sister called him "Fatty" and he got so angry he picked up a clump of mud and threw it at her. His aim was off and the clump hit my daughter in the eye instead. She screamed in pain. Back in the house Alice and I washed out my daughter's eye as best we could. But there was more damage than we could mend ourselves, so I packed her off, still screaming, to our pediatrician's office. Her entire eye had been scratched by the mudball.

The pediatrician referred her to an ophthalmologist, who had my daughter return to his office daily for one week. Although she ended up with no vision problems, her eye was permanently scarred by the mud. When Richie heard of this, his response was to throw up. When he came to our house to apologize, his eyes were filled with tears.

In many ways he was such a likable kid it was impossible to stay angry with him for very long.

As Richie moved through the grades in elementary school, I picked up more and more reports about his behavior. Apparently, his teachers had no idea what to do with him.

It surprised me that no one tested him for any learning disabilities or gave appropriate credence to his problems with hyperactivity, distractibility, and impulsivity. However, this was in the days prior to Public Law 94-142 (later changed to Individuals with Disabilities Education Act or IDEA). Fortunately, a lot has changed since the enactment of that federal law. Richie's parents traipsed with him from one specialist to another—pediatrician, ophthalmologist, neurologist, audiologist, psychologist, and psychiatrist. No one seemed to have any answers.

No one, I think, did more harm to Richie than the psychologist who told his mother that she was to blame for his poor behavior and troubles in school. "You do not have a good relationship with your son," he told her, "and until you can get rid of the hostile feelings you harbor toward him, you can expect a continuation of the behavior that's driving your whole family berserk."

Alice choked back tears as she related this to me. I looked at her in astonishment and said, "My God, how could you possibly *not* have negative feelings toward such a child? He never slows down, never gives you a break, is constantly into something or other. If I were his mother, I'd be a lot more upset with him than you are. At times I think I'd want to break his neck!"

We both laughed, but we knew that Richie's case was no laughing matter.

Just as we were finishing our laugh, we heard a crash. As we looked across the yard, we saw glass smashing to the ground. Richie had just broken his bedroom window!

Such incidents were commonplace. Earlier that week his mother had sent him to his room for being too aggressive with the other children. The week before he had been grounded for peeling wallpaper off the walls. Another time he had pried up some of the floorboards when he was confined to his bedroom. With Richie it was just one outrageous thing after another.

A few months after Alice had been told by the psychologist that her poor relationship with her son was the root cause of his wildness, she went into a deep depression and was referred to a psychiatrist. I felt that Richie's psychologist should have been the one to pay Alice's psychiatric bills.

A neighbor told me one day that she'd heard Richie was going to be expelled from school if his behavior did not improve immediately. By this time Richie was spending much of his school day in the principal's office because the classroom teachers couldn't control his behavior. If he wasn't controllable in third grade, what on earth would his behavior be like in, say, ninth grade?

By this point I had begun to suspect that learning disabilities were at the heart of Richie's behavioral problems. Alice's son had had psychological evaluations, but no learning disabilities testing.

I asked his parents if I could help them with such tests, and they readily agreed. They looked so hopeful I was sorry I hadn't mustered my courage to suggest such testing much earlier. Why no authority at Richie's school had ordered up similar tests was hard to understand.

Richie came to my home the following Saturday for the tests. He thought he was coming to help me with a graduate class I was taking in which I was required to administer certain tests. I was stunned to see how many transpositions and reversals appeared in his writing. Richie was then in third grade, but he spelled on a first-grade level while reading on a fifth-grade level.

One test I administered was the Slingerland Screening Test for Identifying Specific Language Disabilities. This is an informal test to see if additional, more precise, testing needs to be done. The test guide states, however, that if a subject makes more than twelve errors, he needs further testing. Richie made eighty-three errors. A few of those errors concerned reading, but the lion's share were spelling mistakes.

Richie's teachers had been insisting that if he could read, he could spell—if he really wanted to. They were far from realizing that different processes are required for reading and spelling. I wondered how many other children had not been referred for testing of either reading or spelling, simply because they could do one or the other fairly well, but were weak in the other skill. Richie was certainly a case in point.

During the testing at my home I noticed that Richie was distracted by any noise, regardless of how soft it was or from how far away it came. His attention span was extremely short, and at every second he had some part of his body in motion. If his hands weren't moving, his feet were swinging under the table. Sometimes his head bobbed up and down as he wrote; at other times, when apparently deep in thought, he hummed to himself.

Two weeks later I spoke with his parents about the test results. Richie was severely dyslexic with an above average IQ. He was actually much more intelligent than his test scores indicated, but he couldn't score well because of his short attention span and his hyperactivity. Today he would be labeled ADHD (attention deficit hyperactivity disorder).

Richie certainly had the classic signs of dyslexia:

1. Reversals in mathematics (6/9);
2. Transpositions in mathematics (53/35);
3. Rotation of directional signs for addition and multiplication (43x3=46);
4. Reversals in spelling (*b*/*d*);
5. Transposals in spelling (*for*/*from*);
6. Bizarre spelling of words he had seen many times (*here*/*heir*, *where*/*whair*, *girl*/*grill*);
7. Ability to learn to spell some words with no carryover in writing them;
8. Ability to spell words orally with no difficulty;
9. Nearly illegible handwriting;
10. Difficulty reading from left to right consistently;
11. Severe discrepancy between ability and achievement.

I recommended that Richie be referred to his school system and placed in a Learning Disabilities classroom as soon as possible. And it should, I strongly suggested, be a full-time placement until he improved enough to function satisfactorily in a regular classroom.

Richie's parents agreed to pursue having him placed in an LD class. Unfortunately, his school did not then have an LD teacher. After an unproductive meeting with administrators in the local school district, Richie's father, David, decided to attend a School Board meeting to make his case. When he did so, a board member looked sternly at David and said, "Sir, this is an upper-middle-class community. We have children from intelligent, well-educated families in our schools, and we do not have a need for anything like LD teachers."

David informed that gentleman that both he and his wife were Phi Beta Kappa and had completed graduate and professional schools. When David finished speaking, I am sure the board member regretted his *faux pas*. I only regret I wasn't there to cheer.

Despite his parents' persistence, Richie's school did not add an LD teacher.

At the time I was principal of a learning disabilities center associated with the city school system. I asked the assistant superintendent if Richie could attend the center and pay tuition, since he hailed from a nearby county. The response was "yes," and Richie shifted into a new academic gear—one that we all hoped would get him "on track."

Richie spent several years at the LD center. I gave him a ride to school each day, and in my car, where we chatted amiably, he was a precious, freckle-faced cherub whose smile was contagious. Yet each day as we arrived at the center, I watched him change from a delightful car companion to a hostile, hyperactive menace ever on the prowl for ways to cause trouble. In an earlier day he would have been the "problem student" who put frogs in the teacher's desk or dipped the pig tails of the girl sitting in front of him into his inkwell—all the while looking perfectly innocent.

The first year at the center Richie learned almost nothing. He reminded me of a puppy that needed to be left alone to lick its wounds. So we did just that. We let Richie know we cared about him, but did not pressure him to "produce" the way we did with some of the other children. He couldn't have taken it. After a year, Richie began to participate actively in his remedial sessions. He started to enjoy learning and to smile more often.

I can't say his behavior was perfect, but it was vastly improved. Richie had learned he could trust us. That was a big step.

The only teaching method that seemed to work with Richie was the Orton-Gillingham approach. The Simultaneous Oral Spelling (S.O.S.) technique was perfect for him because it made the writing process less complex. This technique prescribes the following steps:

1. The teacher says the spelling word;
2. The student repeats the word;
3. The student says the sounds of the individual letters (if necessary);
4. The student says the names of the letters in the word;
5. The student writes the word and reads the word.

The center also taught Richie the linkages in the Orton-Gillingham approach. This meant he learned to relate each letter to a concrete object, and he repeated daily the name of the letter (*b*), the object that would remind him of the sound (boy), and the letter sound (/*b*/). He also pronounced the sounds and names of combinations of letters (/*br*/ *br*; /*sh*/ *sh*) and would then write the letters.

Dr. Samuel Orton and Anna Gillingham felt that it was possible to correct a student's problems with written language by sending information to the brain through different sensory channels. The purpose here is to strengthen the weak linkages and to improve the strong linkages. For example, the information of letter/sound correspondence may be received visually (seeing a letter), auditorially (saying/hearing the sound) and/or kinesthetically (writing the letter). This multi-sensory approach—such as hearing a word and then writing it—improves the smoothness of the flow of information from one sensory channel to another.

Reading, spelling, handwriting, and written language were taught simultaneously at the center. Richie spelled what he read, wrote about what he read, and practiced handwriting the same material. Thus he had more repetition in learning—and the same information went to the brain through a variety of channels.

The truth is, it just makes more sense to use an integrated approach to reading, spelling, and handwriting for LD students.

Perhaps publishers can sell more when teachers use separate books for each skill, but such a practice has never seemed wise to me. Experience has shown me that children do better when teaching materials for the separate skills reinforce one another.

Richie spent many months sheltered in the LD center, a safe and secure place for students with learning difficulties. Time passed, however, and the day arrived when he had to leave the center and go to high school.

There he found limited support for his particular problems. He had to be in the mainstream classroom most of the time. None of his high-school teachers seemed to understand his language difficulties. When Alice explained to the teachers that Richie had dyslexia and dysgraphia, they did everything but ask if he had been inoculated for those diseases. Several asked if he was retarded.

Because writing was very laborious for him, one morning Richie found he was not ready to turn in a mid-term exam in Social Studies at the period's end. His teacher stood in front of Richie's desk and snarled, "Don't tell me you haven't finished your exam, Richie. I guess you know more than anyone else in here. Is that why you haven't finished yet?" Richie could feel his face flush. He could feel the anger surging up inside. After the teacher made other rude comments, Richie stood up, towering over the teacher by a full foot. He balled up his test and threw it on the floor, then strode dramatically to the door and slammed it behind him as he left the classroom.

Richie had studied for that test. He knew all the answers— orally. But he couldn't get them down on paper properly and in time. The longer he worked on the test, the more frustrated he grew. Soon his concentration went to pieces. He ended up leaving much of the test blank. A recommendation that Richie be given oral tests had gone unheeded. Therefore his grades were poor. Worse, some of his old aggressive behavior began to re-emerge after Richie experienced failure for a few months in high school.

One day I stopped by a neighborhood grocery to pick up a few things for dinner. I spotted several tough-looking boys standing around outside. Inside, I found Richie; he was walking up and down the aisles furtively. When he saw me, his face turned crimson, so I figured he probably was up to no good. Eventually, he stepped outdoors with his provisions—without passing through the checkout counter. He handed over everything he had pilfered to the ruffians outside. The tough boys laughed, then rode off on their motorcycles, leaving Richie behind. My heart ached for this young man who wanted so desperately to be accepted.

Success eluded Richie in high school. He rarely had an understanding teacher. Even the help he received in the LD room at the school was limited, because the teacher was usually only provisionally certified and had scant knowledge of Richie's particular difficulties. The school provided him with absolutely no remedial work in spelling and writing.

Richie went through high school sitting in basic classes, with no regard for his above-average intelligence. He was separated from his neighborhood friends, because they were all in college prep classes. Before long, Richie's only companions were boys who were not a positive influence on him. He began to feel uncomfortable around successful students and deliberately sought out alienated peers. He slid into abusing alcohol and taking drugs. As time passed he ignored his parents' curfew and stayed out as long as he pleased. When his parents took away his driver's license, he drove without one. Ordered to remain confined to the house, he climbed out a bedroom window to join his questionable buddies. Alice and David were frantic. Richie was out of control and they didn't know what to do next.

Only once in his four years of high school did Richie come home with any positive comment written on his report card. That one time, though, he handed the report card to his mother and said, "Take a look at what my teacher said about me!" Alice was touched to see her six-foot-one teenage son standing proud. She wondered what high school could have been like for him if more teachers had shown some appreciation of her son.

The saving grace for Richie, however, was the vocational technical program at the school. There Richie was assigned to work with a Mr. Jones, a man who had made a craft of restoring old houses. This talented and good-natured man helped Richie and a friend of his, Joe, to acquire skills in carpentry. Alice noticed that her son was much more relaxed after a few hours of working with wood. Richie liked Mr. Jones, and very fortunately for Richie, the feeling was mutual. Mr. Jones offered Richie a job in his house-restoration firm upon graduation. Eagerly, Richie accepted. Now he had a hope: to become a master carpenter.

Carpentry was Richie's first step back into the sunlight. Measuring, sawing, and hammering helped him expend some of his limitless energy in a productive fashion.

Gradually, he felt better and better, both physically and emotionally. No longer did he act like a caged animal looking for someone to attack. Life was looking up.

Then he met Alison. When he was with Alison, Richie felt great about himself. He stopped riding roughshod over all the rules at home. Surprised and relieved, his parents felt that they had gained back a son.

During Richie's last year of high school, Alice called to tell me that Richie and Alison were engaged to be married. Richie's fiancée came from a very successful family; she seemed to be intelligent and caring. The couple were expecting a baby.

After plans for the wedding were made final, Alison had a miscarriage. Like others who knew Richie well, I mistakenly thought that the wedding would now be forgotten, but it occurred just as planned. Many acquaintances gave the marriage a few months at best. Richie had not seemed to understand the meaning of responsibility during his high-school career. It was hard to think of him behaving well as a husband.

Because of money being tight, Alison and Richie had to live

with Richie's parents until they could both graduate, get work, and achieve some financial independence.

Soon after Richie's wedding, I moved with my family to another state. When my husband and I were back in our old town, we visited with Richie's parents for a weekend. There were slightly muffled arguments between Richie and almost everyone else in the household going on rather constantly. Doors slammed all over the place. The room we stayed in had a large hole in the wall. Alice apologized for the hole, saying Richie had recently put his fist through the wall. After our stressful weekend, I was convinced that Richie's marriage to Alison would be brief.

Events proved me wrong.

Richie got his high school diploma, though by the skin of his teeth, and then went to work for Mr. Jones as a carpenter's apprentice. Alison had work in a doctor's office.

It turned out that Alison was exactly what Richie needed. She has been a good and stabilizing influence on him. More than anyone else I know, Alison has always been accepting of Richie's problems. And she has worked diligently with him to help him find ways of letting off steam. Alison is a very special person. But—and we mustn't overlook this—so is Richie.

Richie and his friend Joe worked for Mr. Jones for six years until they had saved enough to start their own company. Alison kept the books. The company grew and became quite successful. Today Richie and Joe have three crews and it's all they can do to cope with the work orders that roll in. Richie is very respected in the construction industry in his area, not only for his financial success but also, and especially, for the pride he takes in the quality of work his company produces. He is known now for his careful attention to details, and told me recently, "I'd rather lose money on a job than charge somebody for something that isn't done right."

Using his hyperactivity in a positive way has proven quite profitable for Richie. That inner welling up of an overabundance of energy that once caused so much havoc in his life now contributes to his success in the construction business. Also, when Richie returns home after a day at work, he is physically tired and thus able to relax. He reads for pleasure now, something he did not do while in school, because there he couldn't sit still long enough and his mind was always racing on ahead of him.

Richie and Alison recently had their first child, Richie Jr. They are good parents. Richie takes an active role in caring for his son. Despite a somewhat rocky beginning, he and Alison have developed an unusually solid marriage. From what I can see, they communicate extremely well. And at this writing Richie was in the process of building the dream home that he and Alison had designed together.

Today Richie has a comfortable relationship with his parents. They are almost ecstatic that Richie is finally happy, responsible, and successful. At times they have to pinch themselves to realize that their son is no longer a serious problem for them and others, that instead he is a source of great pride and joy.

Just a few short years ago neither I nor anyone else who knew Richie would have guessed that his story could have a happy ending. But this saga, initially anguishing and now joyful, isn't over yet. Richie plans to increase the size of his business. As Richie Jr. moves through his childhood, Richie will be there to support him emotionally and academically. If the boy has inherited dyslexia and/or ADHD, Richie will see to it that his son receives the appropriate education which the Individuals with Disabilities Education Act (IDEA) guarantees. For now, at age three, Richie Jr. does not appear to be hyperactive, and for that everyone in his family is grateful.

At many points during Richie's growing up I would have sworn his chances for a happy, fulfilling life were slim. With the right support, however, positive reform is possible. May this story be a source of hope to parents and children plagued by learning difficulties and problems with ADHD that have made them feel there is no hope.

chapter 3

cornelius

WHY, I WONDERED, did the associate coach of the football team want to talk with me on this sunny day in August? Settling himself into the chair I offered as he entered my office, Coach Joe Brown smiled at me and took an unusually direct approach:

"Dr. Guyer, I'll get right to the point. I have a young man on the team, a defensive lineman, who is a freshman with a unique background. For one thing, I've just learned that he went through his school system diagnosed as mentally retarded. I'll eat my hat if he really is.

"We wouldn't have recruited him, of course, if we'd thought he was mentally retarded, but now that we are aware of this designation, we need to know what this player's potential is."

I nodded an "of course."

"This young man," Coach Brown continued, "Cornelius Smith is his name, has a very good speaking vocabulary. I just don't believe he would have such a vocabulary if he were actually mentally retarded, would he? He's also African American, lived in a small rural town, and he comes from a family that is not educated. He couldn't overcome those obstacles, acquire excellent language skills and good general knowledge and still be retarded, could he?"

"That would be very unlikely," I conceded.

"There's something else… pretty disturbing. After Cornelius had been here a few days, I told him we'd need to start thinking about the classes he would take in the fall. Cornelius just looked at me in a panic. 'Classes?!' he said. 'I can't take any classes, Coach. I can't read anything to speak of. Everything I know I've learned by just listening or watching. I thought I could just play football and not take classes right away.'

"I told this young man he would have to take eight classes the first year and maintain a C average. Cornelius looked as me as if he were going to be sick."

"Would your Cornelius be willing to work hard?" I asked.

"Yes, I think so, but I can't be sure. He has excellent recommendations from his teachers in high school. That's about all I can tell you, except that he has followed my instructions to the letter so far; that's more than I can say for some of the other boys on the team."

Coach Brown's brow furrowed. He started to add something, hesitated, and then tried again. "Dr. Guyer... I... ah, I... well, I wanted to mention something else about Cornelius."

"Oh? There's more?"

"Yes. I'm not, of course, a reading teacher or anything, and I probably should stick to football, but I've noticed some signs of dyslexia in Cornelius... at least, I think they're signs. He reverses a lot of letters when he writes. Also, in football practice he mixes up right and left. Aren't those signs of dyslexia?"

"They can be. It's certainly worth looking into, Coach," I responded. I looked at this middle-aged football coach with new respect. He had spotted symptoms in this young man's style of writing and acting that had been missed, apparently, by teachers in twelve years of public schooling. Over the years in my future dealings with Coach Brown, I came to understand just how perceptive he was. Seldom, when he referred a student to me, did he make an incorrect assumption of the underlying cause of the student's academic problems. My thought was, "We need more coaches — and teachers — like Coach Brown."

When Cornelius arrived for testing, I was struck by how handsome he was. He had close-shaven hair, large, expressive brown

eyes and an infectious smile. When Cornelius smiled, it was difficult not to smile back. He stood six feet four inches tall and his
muscles showed he made frequent use of the university's weight-
lifting equipment and workout rooms. Probably what I liked most
about him was the expression in his eyes. He radiated kindness and
caring.

I first gave Cornelius the Wechsler Adult Intelligence Scale-
Revised (WAIS-R) and noticed that he reversed numbers frequently.
In spite of the reversal problems, Cornelius scored 119 in IQ. A normal intelligence quotient is approximately one hundred, and the
gifted range begins at 130, so Cornelius clearly was not short of
brains. During testing I observed how anxious he was, so I took
time out frequently to chat with him. I was determined that
Cornelius not score low on this test simply out of uneasiness with
me as the examiner. Perhaps such anxiety had compromised his
scores during testing in high school. If a school psychologist or
other examiner had been at all abrupt or threatening to Cornelius,
the young man might well have skipped answering certain questions or been too rattled to focus on his best answer.

Next we went on to the Woodcock-Johnson Tests of
Achievement. These revealed that Cornelius was reading on a second-grade level. In this test he reversed almost everything that
could be reversed. His spelling and written language skills also registered on a second-grade level. In arithmetic he was functioning
on a high-school level, however—definitely an asset.

Despite all his academic deficits, Cornelius had a positive
demeanor. I wondered how he had achieved this. I got the feeling
it had something to do with his mother, Mary, whom, I was later
to learn, was a very special lady.

The spring before I met Cornelius I had tested another young
man, named Dutch, whose academic dilemma touched me
deeply. He was in the beginning range of genius intelligence,
whereas his reading comprehension was on a beginning high-
school level. His spelling was rather creative, but not impossible.

Cornelius

When I asked Dutch to describe himself to me, he said rather sadly, "I'm just a dumb jock." Being the only person in a successful family who hasn't done well in school is very difficult. Self-esteem suffers daily, and it was understandable that his opinion of himself was quite negative. He had almost given up hope at the tender age of twenty-two. I didn't seem to be able to escape the haunted look I saw in his eyes; I couldn't get Dutch out of my thoughts. I had to do something, I felt, to help him succeed in college.

One night, my husband, Ken, suggested: "Why don't you apply for a Project of Greatest Need Grant?" At our university if a professor felt very strongly that something needed to be implemented or changed, it was possible to apply for such a grant. If selected, the project would be funded by the Marshall University Foundation. With my husband's assistance, I wrote the grant and then hoped for the best. My proposal was selected for funding, and that fall we were able to begin providing tutoring services to students with learning disabilities. I was given one-half release time from my teaching duties, and two graduate assistants were also paid through the grant.

Cornelius and Dutch were to be the first two students enrolled in the H.E.L.P. (Higher Education for Learning Problems) Program at Marshall University. We began working together in the fall, not really knowing what to do, more or less feeling our way.

These two young men had much in common, but in some ways were very dissimilar. Both, for example, were athletes, and both were willing to work hard. Both had IQs significantly higher than average, and both had dyslexia. The differences were that Dutch was a Caucasian raised in a city by two parents who were happily married, and Cornelius was an African-American raised in a rural area by a single parent, his mother. Cornelius' father, however, was always available when Cornelius needed him, and faithfully provided financial support for the family. From what Cornelius told me, his father was also a good role model.

Soon after we launched the program, we accepted another student, and so our graduate assistants had three subjects to help prepare for examinations. It wasn't long before I realized that simply focusing on exam prep was not enough; we also needed to address study skills, memory aids and remedial techniques to enable students to improve their reading and spelling.

At the outset many Marshall professors were concerned that our H.E.L.P. students would not be able to function as quality undergraduate products who would reflect well on the university. This was certainly a reasonable concern. If, however, I could manage to convince the professors that the help we were providing to these students would measurably improve their skills, and their chances for academic success, I felt the level of anxiety among our teaching corps would decrease. Then, too, I believed, the professors who could see measurable results would be much more cooperative with me and my staff. And this proved to be true.

Cornelius began working with a graduate assistant (G.A.) named Sherry in reading and spelling. We had decided to use the Orton-Gillingham approach of teaching individual sounds in words as an aid to spelling, because this approach had been devised especially for the dyslexic student. I had used this method quite successfully in the Richmond city schools. After three weeks of work with Sherry, Cornelius had begun to make progress in both reading and spelling. One day he looked at her as if a light had gone on in his head, and asked, "Do you mean to tell me that every word is made up of individual sounds?"

"Yes," she said, smiling.

"When you read, do you take sounds apart, and when you spell, do you put sounds together? Does that mean that if I can learn to put sounds together and take them apart I can read my books and spell right?"

"Well, that's a bit simplified," Sherry responded. "But in a general sense, yes, that's correct."

"Man! I never knew that words had sounds. I always thought

I had to memorize every word and that words didn't have anything in common. I just couldn't imagine how I was supposed to memorize thousands of words. If only someone had told me a lot earlier that words were made up of sounds!"

That day Cornelius almost floated out of the building.

Other days proved more frustrating. I remember distinctly one day when Sherry was helping Cornelius study for a history test. He seemed so overwhelmed with all he had to put into his head that he couldn't concentrate on anything. He looked like a scared rabbit. As the time approached for him to take that test, his thinking became even more muddled. Sherry recognized that he was in trouble and came to me for advice.

"I don't know what to do, Dr. G. He's just too frightened to focus."

It occurred to me at that moment that perhaps we were asking too much of Cornelius too quickly. Very little had been demanded of him in high school, where he had lettered in four sports and had been all-state in three sports. Cornelius had told me several times that he behaved well in high school and bothered no one. His teachers had just let him sit in class without expecting much of him. They gave him passing grades as a "reward;" in reality, he had learned almost nothing. Now, at the university, he was expected to perform on a level with students who had been in college prep classes for four years in high school. Even the best of tutoring could not overcome that handicap. There were times when Cornelius did very well, but on certain days, like the one in question here, he was ready to pack his bags and go home to his mother.

I took Sherry's place at the table with Cornelius and tried to help him relax. I paused for a moment, not quite knowing what to say. "Cornelius, you've been worried about this History class since the semester began. Can you tell me why?"

"Mrs. G, I've never studied stuff like this before. Before this semester, nobody ever told me anything about the Romans or the

Greeks. I don't know what they're talking about. I feel so lost in that class!"

"Cornelius, if you had lived during that time, would it be easier for you to learn the kinds of things we're asking you to know?"

"Sure. It would be easy then."

I had a clue then as to what we could do. It was at least worth a try. "Cornelius, close your eyes. Let's try a little experiment. You are now living in Rome, and your name is Corleone. Your father is a successful contractor who builds houses. He is a man who has a great deal of integrity, and sometimes the dishonesty of the government is difficult for him to bear. One day a dishonest tax collector, who has already collected taxes from your father once, comes to collect them again. Can you see him?"

"Yes, I can," Cornelius smiled.

"Your father protests and says that he has paid the taxes. He refuses to pay again. The tax collector becomes very angry and has your father put in jail. Now, how would this differ from what might have happened to your father in the United States today if someone tried to collect taxes the second time? I want you to tell what would have happened to your father in Rome, and then say what would have happened to your father here."

Cornelius answered the question without hesitation. I knew that he had learned the information, and it was a matter of getting it back from him. From then on, I instructed his tutors to be sure that in every class they related what was being studied to what Cornelius already knew. After all, isn't association one of the primary ways we learn? This technique worked beautifully. Fortunately, Cornelius visualized very easily, and he could take his visualization to a test with him. This technique has worked with innumerable other students as well. Cornelius was able to make average grades in most of his classes, which was amazing, considering the limitations of his background.

There was a funny twist to Cornelius' improved progress, however; he suddenly had trouble recognizing and accepting himself in his new academic position.

He came into my office one day obviously upset. He slammed his books down on my filing cabinet and glared at me. I was stunned. I didn't recognize in the angry young man before me the Cornelius I was accustomed to seeing.

"Mrs. G, I can't take this *average* business!" he vented.

"I don't understand, Cornelius. What do you mean?"

Cornelius put his hands on his hips and glared at me again. "I'll have you know that I used to be the best failure of anybody, and now I'm just *average!*"

So this was what I had read about in textbooks. I stared at this disgruntled young dyslexic athlete, not knowing how I should respond. Finally, I said, "Why don't you sit down and let's talk for awhile?"

Sigh… "Okay, Mrs. G."

"Cornelius, what kind of future does the best failure in town have? Who wants to hire the best failure? Would you if you were doing the hiring?"

He looked at the floor a little sheepishly, realizing what he had said and how it had sounded.

"Cornelius, you have had so many changes in your life during the last year, and I know it has been difficult for you to adjust to all of them. Do you trust me?"

He nodded affirmatively, his eyes a little misty.

"If you continue to work as hard as you have been doing, continue to go to class regularly and come to tutoring faithfully, I believe you can eventually be a better-than-average student. Your reading and spelling are certainly improving. Can't you see a difference in your skills?"

"Yes, Ma'am." A timid smile creased the edges of his mouth.

Cornelius stood up, shook my hand, and picked up his scattered books. He winked at me as he left my office. I knew we were over the hump.

He often came to my office after that just to unload the day's frustration or sometimes just for a friendly chat. His visits became something I looked forward to. One day he began talking with the chairman of the Special Education Department, and that gentleman was impressed with how personable Cornelius was. He told Cornelius how much he enjoyed watching him play football. Cornelius was delighted. That experience boosted his morale for several weeks. During one of their conversations, the chairman mentioned that he was trying to sell his Volkswagen "bug." Cornelius was very interested. He called his father, who agreed to give his son the money he needed for the purchase. Seeing the tall, athletically built Cornelius drive around in such a small car became one of my favorite memories of him. Whenever he saw me, he always honked, rolled down the window, and yelled, "Hey, Mrs. G, it's me, Cornelius!" I always returned the greeting with some exaggerated waving, and we both laughed.

My other favorite memory occurred two years after our first meeting. I entered the Special Education office one day, and Cornelius was sitting in the waiting room. He was reading the school newspaper, not just looking at the pictures. I could tell that he was reading the words by the expression on his face. There were no pictures on the page he was reading. I stopped dead in my tracks and stared. Then I felt myself break out in a broad grin. This was the kind of result that could make a teacher's day—or even her year!

When I first met Cornelius, he told me of a heartbreaking experience he had with the football team. They had an out-of-town game, and whenever they went out to eat dinner, the boys were required to wear suits. Cornelius related, "I had on my best suit, and I was feeling like I was Somebody, Mrs. G. We sat down to order our dinner in this gorgeous restaurant. You shoulda seen it! It was neat! Wow! Then some man passed around the menus at my table. When everyone was looking at the menus, one of the guys at my table said very loudly, 'Hey, Cornelius. What are you doing, man? You're reading the menu upside down! You can't read anything that way! I can't believe you're doing that.'" Cornelius said he wanted to die on the spot. He was humiliated beyond words. For days afterward he felt depressed because the whole football team, even the coaches, had heard what his "friend" had said about how he'd been holding the menu. After that, Cornelius told me, he never looked at a menu. He listened carefully to what the person next to him ordered, and then said, "That sounds pretty good. I believe I'll have that, too."

He told me, however, "Sometimes what I ordered that way was downright nasty. Ugh! I had a hard time eating some of it. If I could just have read the menu, I could have gotten what I wanted."

The next fall Cornelius came by my office one Monday morning after class. "Mrs. G, I gotta talk to you. This was a big weekend for me."

"Really, Cornelius? What happened? I'm all ears."

He smiled proudly, savoring every moment. "I took my girlfriend to a restaurant this weekend. But that isn't the best part. I read the menu all by myself, right side up. I read everything I ordered. My girlfriend was so proud of me, and I was proud of me. What a good feeling. I made up my mind at that awful dinner with the football team that I was going to learn how to read well enough to read a menu. And I have. Thanks, Mrs. G." I got a powerful bear hug that day, a big day not only for Cornelius but also for me. I'll never forget it as long as I live.

However, after that experience, things began to deteriorate for Cornelius for awhile. His girlfriend became pregnant, and he decided that they should get married. The trials of married life soon began to wear on him. After their son was born, he often seemed to be the one who walked the baby at night, and then he was exhausted the next day. Sometimes he arrived at school too tired to think.

There were times when Cornelius didn't come for tutoring sessions. I finally called Coach Brown to ask for help. He could always find Cornelius and would bring him over to our building.

He and Cornelius seemed to have a good relationship. The young man seemed to understand that the coach had his best interests at heart when he tracked him down.

Gradually, Cornelius became adjusted to being a husband, father, student, athlete, dyslexic, and even a public speaker. I often asked him to speak to a class I was teaching or to visit a school in the area. He was able to share his experiences with a sense of humor that endeared him to others. Whenever he spoke, the audience laughed a great deal. He could tell the most amusing stories about himself. I began to realize that sometimes he used humor as a shield behind which he could hide his tears.

By and by Cornelius completed the classes for his degree in education. And, by this time, he was able to read his textbooks, though slowly. He had come so far.

One setback that he experienced occurred when the new football coach arrived. This coach's personality was completely different from Coach Brown's. He was a rather negative person, from my perspective, and I heard that he did a lot of criticizing of the players in front of other people. I saw him yelling at Cornelius during a football game, ridiculing him for some play he had missed. Throughout Cornelius's life, the only thing he had done well was to participate in sports. He was regarded by everyone as an exceptional athlete. With the new coach's attitude, Cornelius became more depressed by the day. I took it as long as I could, and then made an appointment with the coach to talk with him about Cornelius. I was determined to try to stop the ridiculing. To the best of my ability, I explained to the coach and his assistant that Cornelius, because of his problems with self-esteem, needed to be complimented, not ridiculed. I'm not sure the coach and the assistant really understood what I said that day, but their treatment of Cornelius did improve.

When it was time for Cornelius to begin student teaching, I held my breath. This would be the supreme challenge. Was Cornelius up to this? Only time would tell. He and I discussed how he could survive as a dyslexic in the classroom. We agreed that he would not write on the chalk board. Instead, he would use overhead transparencies, and he would have each one checked for spelling before he used it in class. Lecturing was no problem for him since he was a verbal person. It was written language that gave him trouble. He purchased a spell checker that fit in his shirt pocket, and he used it whenever he needed help. Of course, there were words that stumped the spell checker. We suggested that he make friends with someone in his classes who would be able to help him with spelling. If he completed his overhead transparencies in advance, the only immediate spelling assistance he should need would be for impromptu notes. We talked about how he could get students to write on the board instead of his doing it. Then, if all else failed, and he had a spelling problem, or a reversal problem, he decided how he would tell the class that he had dyslexia. This eventuality did in fact occur. His supervising teacher told me that Cornelius did an excellent job of telling the class about his lifelong bouts with dyslexia. Apparently, he gave hope to many of his students who had a variety of learning problems themselves. They began to realize that there was some possibility that they could succeed as well.

Cornelius was able to complete his student teaching, but not the first semester. He, his supervising teacher, and his university supervisor all agreed that it would be wise to take a second semester of student teaching. We all wanted to be absolutely sure that Cornelius would be a good teacher when he graduated and a credit to his profession. He wanted that more than anyone else, and whatever was suggested, he did. The next semester he performed on a more skillful level. It was easy to see that he was pleased with his performance. He was very glad that he had repeated the semester.

The semester he graduated was exciting for Cornelius's entire family. He was the first person in his family to graduate from college, and relatives from far and near arrived for the graduation exercises. I didn't see him when I took my place with the faculty and entered the auditorium; however, that night the eleven o'clock news carried a story on the Marshall University graduation. I was delighted to see that Cornelius was one of the graduates who was featured. Surely no one in the auditorium had overcome more than this bright young man. I wondered how many college graduates had entered college able to read virtually nothing. Cornelius had done this, and he was graduating with the ability to read his textbooks. His spelling was fairly good unless he was rushed, such as writing a note to someone. He knew exactly how to deal with dyslexia, and it was wise to have planned his responses in advance.

That night I went to bed smiling. I pictured Cornelius, on his first job, teaching in a small town. He would be, I was sure, an excellent role model for teenage boys, especially those inclined toward trouble. I felt certain that he could do a great deal of good during his teaching career. I fell asleep grateful for the small part I played in his success. There were others, of course, who contributed immeasurably. Coach Brown made it all possible by being so perceptive and referring Cornelius for testing when he first arrived on campus. Without Coach Brown, Cornelius could have failed miserably, flunked out of college, and joined young men on the street corners with nothing to do. Thanks too were due to the tireless tutors who gave him many hours of help that went far beyond what was required of them; due also to many of his professors who did everything possible to help him.

Cornelius deserves a great deal of credit as well. There were many times when he was tempted to throw in the towel and go home where everything was "safe." Today I am confident that he is grateful he stayed and persevered to reach graduation and the threshold of a teaching career. Down through the years Cornelius will multiply his own success through his encouragement of students to hurdle the obstacles barring their way, so that they too can lead rewarding, productive lives.

chapter 4

andy

ANDY, A TALL, slim young man with dimples, managed a half smile as he peered at me. He had a searching look in his eyes. I could sense he had been hurt many times. He looked at me for a few seconds, then shifted his glance to the floor.

Although quiet, Andy had a sophistication one seldom sees in a high school senior. When I directed questions to him, he accepted them without hesitation and answered intelligently, clearly, and with complete sentences.

Andy and his parents were looking for a college with a good support program for learning disabled students. They had come here to Marshall's H.E.L.P. Program on the recommendation of a consultant who had caught one of our presentations at a national conference.

I explained the basic methods and goals of the H.E.L.P. Program to Andy and his mother; then a student and a tutor related their personal experiences of the dyslexic's educational battlefield. Andy remained very quiet, not atypical of many of our prospective students. His mother asked the questions, though there was no hostility between mother and teenage son as is so often the case when dyslexia is an issue. These two had a positive relationship, and the conversation definitely indicated Andy's mother was his greatest supporter.

A few weeks later I received a call from Andy's father, Brian Anderson, a well-known businessman and president of an international company. He told me his wife and son considered our program at the top of their list. He added, "I want to come over and see for myself."

I was impressed. This busy and very successful father wanted to take the time to visit his son's prospective college. Few fathers seem willing to do that. Most successful men I have known expect their wives to do almost everything involving the children. "My husband just doesn't have time for this sort of thing," is a comment I've heard from many women. I wonder how that makes the children feel.

While Mr. Anderson learned about H.E.L.P. from me, I learned about Andy's background and learning problems. Before Andy began kindergarten, he was a carefree child who brought laughter into the lives of those around him. His vibrant personality made him popular with everyone. His mother first became concerned when Andy's sister, Blain, eighteen months younger, became interested in magnetic letters on the refrigerator. By age three Blain was very skilled at naming the letters and arranging them into words on the metallic surface. Andy, however, was still confusing *b* for *d* and 6 for 9 when he enrolled in kindergarten. He knew almost nothing about the alphabet. However, Andy did ask intelligent questions and had an excellent vocabulary.

Although he had a skilled, experienced teacher, Andy did not do well in kindergarten. On the teacher's recommendation, Andy repeated kindergarten the following year. His new teacher was young and inexperienced. Before long Andy began to complain that school was boring. Mrs. Anderson asked the teacher if Andy might have a reading problem. The teacher thought for a moment and then said, "I really don't know why you're so concerned. Some children just learn more slowly than others."

When Mr. Anderson came home from work, his wife met him in the hall. "Brian, I'm really worried about Andy. I don't like his new teacher at all. I don't think she knows much about teaching. And I don' t think she really cares about Andy."

Mr. Anderson frowned. "I was afraid of this. Our only son. Surely he can be happy in school. What did she say we should do?"

"Nothing. I asked her if she thought we should have Andy tested. She said she didn't see any point. She doesn't think there's a problem. But you know very well Blain is way ahead of Andy and she's a year and a half younger."

"Please go to the principal and tell him we want Andy tested."

Mr. Anderson was accustomed to having his orders carried out, and the principal had Andy tested by someone at the school. The testing, which was not thorough, indicated Andy was performing in the average range compared with other children his age. Andy's parents, frustrated, continued to worry. Reading problems were not their area of expertise, however. They didn't trust the teacher or respect her, but they didn't know what else to do. I think if truth be told, a lot of parents find themselves in this predicament.

When Andy entered first grade and still hadn't improved, his parents took him to a university reading center to be evaluated. Brian and Constance were concerned that Andy still confused some letters and numbers, but they were especially worried that he wasn't reading at all. The primary outcome of the testing was an eye examination.

"Nothing wrong with this young man's eyes," the ophthalmologist stated. "They're in perfect condition. If he's having a problem with reading, his eyes don't have anything to do with it."

As Andy finished first grade, his parents were even more concerned about his failure to read. More testing showed he did read on a first grade level, but his reading was very poor. Although Andy made frequent reversals and transpositions throughout the testing, as well as several gross errors, no one at the school suggested more testing. Brian and Constance had a host of questions:

How can our son be doing so badly when he seems to be so intelligent?

Why can't he read better?

Is it true he isn't trying hard enough?
Should we punish him after school?
Why is Andy so different from his sister?

Andy's parents asked themselves such questions every day. But no one seemed to have any answers for them.

When Andy began second grade he was tested privately and finally diagnosed as having a learning disability. His parents enrolled him in Willowbrook, a small private school for children with learning disabilities. The school put just four children in each class in very small rooms with no windows. The school advertised a multi-sensory approach, but Andy seemed to participate mostly in rote learning. He advanced very little during the next few years. Brian and Constance felt he wasn't being challenged at all. Andy, in fact, was bored. He wasn't coming home crying or even visibly upset, but he definitely was unhappy. They seldom saw him smile anymore when he talked about school, while Blain was doing very well in school. What could they do?

By fifth grade Constance began to notice that her son, once so entertaining and smiling, always looked sad. She asked him, "Where have your dimples gone? I never see them anymore." In a pensive mood Constance sometimes reminisced about her elder child, a boy who used to be so happy and cheerful. She was amazed at how his personality had changed. Going to school had certainly made a difference in Andy, and it wasn't a good difference. In addition to losing his smile, Andy became withdrawn. It was hard to get him to respond to anything. Constance believed he withdrew to protect himself from being hurt anymore. She worked hard to help her son, but nothing seemed to work. Constance and her husband had achieved great success in the business world, but where their son's education was concerned, they felt like complete failures.

One evening when Andy was ten years old he sat at the kitchen table trying to read words such as *cat, fat, rat*. His mother walked through the room and noticed her son was having difficulty.

"The word is 'cat,' Andrew."

Andy looked at her in exasperation and screamed, "I hate these stupid words! I've been trying to read them ever since I can remember. I'll still be trying in fifty years." He put his head on his folded arms and wept bitter tears. Constance never forgot that moment, and never stopped trying to find Andy the help he needed.

During grades five and six Andy attended a more challenging university laboratory school. His new classmates seemed more intelligent than the previous ones. Andy still had academic problems, but in the new, stimulating environment he was learning something. Before that time Andy felt he had no real exposure to education.

Testing at the lab school revealed that Andy read on a beginning third grade level and spelled below a second grade level. That wasn't much to show for the many hours of individual assistance he had received during and after school for the last six years. Also, every summer Andy attended a camp for six weeks. He had a good time, but he also received remedial help in language arts. Then for three weeks the family vacationed in New England where a tutor taught him spelling using the Orton-Gillingham approach. He seemed to make some progress during these three-week sessions, but they were over too quickly.

For grades seven and eight Andy transferred back to Willowbrook. This time the school was willing to make some exceptions, including oral examinations, photocopying classmates' notes, access to a resource room for testing, and limited modification of curriculum in foreign language, English, and mathematics.

Constance felt Andy's serious learning problem affected everything he did. She believed Andy was low man on the totem pole in his circle of friends. His friends seemed to see him as "different," partly because Andy had such a poor self-concept and saw himself as different. If only he could have remained the exuberant person who entered kindergarten instead of becoming a frustrated teenager. One good outlet for frustration was helping his father on their farm on weekends. It was good for Andy to see positive results from his efforts. Also, his father was an avid big game hunter and introduced his son to this sport at an early age. The two of them traveled together to Africa, Alaska, Canada, Mexico, and British Columbia on big game hunts. These expeditions surpassed anything his friends could recount and boosted Andy's low self-esteem. Andy lived for the times when he and his father went on an expedition.

One day Andy was playing with his friends after school when one of them, using Andy's BB gun, shot a hole through a window of the sun porch. They immediately began discussing who should take the blame. It was decided that Andy would say he had fired the gun, even though he hadn't. Taking the rap for a buddy was, evidently, yet another way Andy tried to win approval in his group. Andy's father was furious because he knew his son was an expert marksman and could only have hit the window deliberately. Andy was grounded for one month. There would be no hunting, no skating, no television. There would be nothing but school and tutoring. Eventually, Andy told his father he had not fired the shot and arrangements were made for the boys involved to work off the cost of replacing the broken glass.

When Andy was in the seventh grade, Constance told her husband one evening, "Brian, we've got to do something about Andy. He's a nonreader for all practical purposes, and even worse, he always looks so sad. Do you remember the last time he smiled?"

Brian shrugged his shoulders and looked resigned. "I don't know what we can do that we haven't already done."

"If only he could do better in school. Can't we find a tutor who can help him more?"

Brian agreed they would try. And indeed they were able to find an excellent tutor who worked with Andy from seven to nine o'clock every evening. During their sessions Andy was reserved.

His tutor said he seemed "uninspired," and sometimes he became very sleepy. Andy dreaded the arrival of seven o'clock. He knew he wasn't trying very hard, but what was the use? When he did try, he failed just as much as when he didn't. His teachers were always telling him to try harder, even when he had studied for hours. Why waste all that energy, anyway? Andy had already decided he was just too dumb to learn. As far as he could see, school hadn't changed since the first day. He still couldn't read, his writing looked like chicken scratches, and he continued to confuse numbers and the signs for addition and multiplication. But Andy's tutor was very dedicated, and Andy's grades were fairly good; the tutor, however, was actually doing some of his work for him rather than helping him do it, so Andy didn't learn as much as he should have. In all fairness to the tutor, by the time Andy saw her, he was so tired it was hard for him to concentrate. He just wanted to be left alone.

During his high school years Andy enjoyed riding motorcycles and big game hunting, and playing basketball in the backyard. He was not in a tight circle of friends, partly because of the time tutoring required. Andy once told me, " I was more of a loner than anyone else in my school. I liked the kids, but I didn't have time for the activities they always liked to do. Most of all, I felt like I was different from them. And I guess, really, I was."

Sometimes Andy's mother found articles in magazines about successful people who had problems learning to read. Andy would always look at them and say, "Why tell me? Who wants to know about this?" Constance felt his hostile attitude was a cover for his hurt feelings.

Andy's tutoring experiences continued to be unpleasant until his parents realized they should let him take the initiative. One day Andy's mother confronted him and said, "Look, I'm tired of having your tutor call me every day, saying you aren't trying. She says you just sit there and look bored. You're old enough that she shouldn't be communicating with me. She should be communicating with you. From now on you're going to drive yourself to your tutoring sessions. And if you're late, you are the one she is going to confront. If you don't try, that's between the two of you. You're old enough to take care of this yourself."

Andy's jaw dropped in surprise. After a moment he said, "Well, okay, if that's what you want. I'll drive myself to tutoring." He looked forward to being able to drive somewhere by himself every day.

Forcing Andy to accept responsibility for his behavior in tutoring sessions was probably what gradually changed his attitude. His tutor noticed that he seemed more alert. He didn't yawn as much as he used to, and he was beginning to ask questions. She began to compliment Andy occasionally and a faint smile crept over his face.

Another difficulty that was resolved very well involved Andy's Chemistry class. Andy received an F on a test and grumbled, "I hate Chemistry!"

Andy's teacher overheard him and asked, "Do you really hate Chemistry?"

"No, I don't really hate Chemistry," he admitted. "The bad grade I just got makes me hate this class."

"Andy, why don't you let me help. I can tell you're capable of doing very well. You're right on the edge of understanding what's going on in here. You just keep missing it by a little bit. I'd be glad to give you some of my time after school and we'll go over this stuff again, only a little slower. How about it?"

The teacher explained, during these private tutoring sessions, everything that had been covered in class. He and Andy met twice a week for the remainder of the semester. His Chemistry teacher made sure Andy had good notes which were easy to read, and Andy took oral tests. Needless to say, his grades in Chemistry soared. This teacher did wonders for Andy's self-esteem.

Fortunately, the school also had a dedicated LD teacher who explained Andy's problem to the other teachers. Apparently, she was a good communicator because she was able to convince most of the teachers to cooperate with his learning disability. Nevertheless, some teachers, unaccustomed to the appropriate ways to accommodate learning disabilities, accused him of submitting work that was not his or of having unfair help on tests when he took advantage of nonstandard methods, such as having material read to him or taking tests orally while other students were dutifully turning in written material. His parents usually went to school two or three times a month to talk with teachers. It wasn't as though Andy enjoyed having a learning disability. Sometimes his friends, too, accused him of passing because he took special tests outside or in the back of the classroom. Of course, this helped to turn the screw one more notch in his bruised self-concept.

When Andy was in the twelfth grade the time came for deciding about college. His parents acquired catalogs for him and tried to interest him in visiting a variety of schools. Andy was evasive. He appeared uninterested. Then his parents remembered the success they had by making Andy responsible for his tutoring sessions. They decided to withdraw from the college decision. They told Andy, "You know we would like for you to go to college. But more importantly, we want you to do what you want to do. If you decide to go to college, then you must make the arrangements yourself. We're willing to help, but it's your decision." This was the right thing to say. Andy began calling schools. He became personally involved in looking for the right college for himself. It was interesting to observe how much more enthusiastic and responsive he became when he was directly involved and took responsibility.

To help Andy find a college with the proper support program, an educational advisory service was engaged. This service required that Andy be tested and evaluated by a psychologist and educational diagnostician. The Wechsler Adult Intelligence Scale-Revised (WAIS-R) revealed that Andy had an IQ in the normal range; however, the psychologist who tested him reported that he thought Andy's true ability was much higher. Test anxiety and severe problems with reversals lowered Andy's scores significantly. Andy's test indicated he had a very short attention span and was very easily distracted. He would have difficulty paying attention in class and concentrating on reading. Today he would be diagnosed as having an attention deficit disorder (ADD) without hyperactivity. One of the tragedies about Andy's education was that he did not have a thorough psychological-educational evaluation until he was considering attending college.

Andy's performance on the achievement tests also indicated severe dyslexia.

Once Andy decided on Marshall University as possibly the best college for him, I received letters from his high school teachers. They were quite complimentary. One said, "Andy seems to try hard to learn. He has respect for authority, and he is a very friendly boy. He is never a behavior problem in school. The only weakness I ever found is his inability to read." Another teacher wrote that Andy worked hard on his school work and had little time for any other activities. She added, "Andy seems to have friends, and I'm sure he doesn't have any enemies. He's a very pleasant young man, and I respect him for what he has been able to accomplish." I thought one of Andy's mathematics teachers made a comment worthy of note when she said, "Andy is very good at working out math problems in his head. He has his own techniques for solving problems which are certainly different from the ways other students solve the problems. He often gets the correct answers by unorthodox methods." I also noted this comment from one of his teachers: "Andy was beginning to assume a leadership role among his peers when he graduated from high school."

After reading the psychologist's report and the letters from his teachers, I could hardly wait to begin working with Andy, who was entering college with a second-grade reading level. Somehow I knew we could make a difference in his life. I don't have this feeling often about a student, but I just knew Andy was going to learn to read and we were going to teach him. I approached this challenge with real anticipation. Seldom had I felt so optimistic about a student upon first introductions.

When Andy arrived for college he was scared. He reminded me of a turtle gingerly poking its head out of its shell to see if it was safe. At the slightest hint of danger, he closed his shell up tight.

Andy's first tutoring session happened to be in remediation. He was not very happy about more remediation in reading and spelling, but I had made it a requirement for being accepted in the H.E.L.P. Program. Andy had to come for five hours per week because of his very low scores in reading and spelling. Coping in college would be much less traumatic if he could learn to improve basic skills. Also, he would have to pass English classes, a prospect which appeared quite slim.

Cathy, an experienced teacher and tutor with a special gift for relating to people, had been selected to work with Andy. She had an endless amount of patience, and her unique sense of humor would be a great asset as she tried to help him. When Cathy reviewed Andy's test records, sampled his writing, and listened to him read, she noticed he reversed and transposed many letters. He sometimes began reading a word at the second syllable, and he often grossly misread words and inserted words he thought would fit the context of the sentences, e.g., substituting "counting" for "computation." A few of Andy's spelling errors in the initial testing when he arrived at college were crcl/circle, doy/boy, dess/dress, orbre/order, and matir/material.

When Andy came for his first remedial tutoring session, he began by saying he was not coming five times a week. He would come three days a week, but that was all. I smiled when Cathy relayed this information to me because she and I had already anticipated his objection and had agreed to compromise with him.

Andy never missed a session, but he made it clear he didn't want to be there. In the beginning there were many deep sighs, refusals to do assignments during the sessions, and frequent comments such as, "I don't know why we are bothering with this—it won't help." He did not hesitate to tell Cathy he thought remediation was a stupid waste of time. "I've been tutored in several states and it has never been worth a hill of beans as far as I'm concerned," he huffed. "All you have to do is listen to me read to tell it's all been a big waste." He sometimes sat with arms folded, as if to say, "Go on, teach me something. I dare you." Cathy, one of the best teachers I have ever met, decided to take the dare. She spent hours trying to find ways to help Andy learn to read and write. Gradually, he began to make progress.

One day Cathy told me in exasperation that she thought Andy might want to have another tutor. She didn't think he liked her. I asked Andy if he wanted to work with someone else, and he grinned. "No. I like Cathy a lot. I'm just trying her out, you know, giving her a hard time. I don't mean anything by it." Yes, I knew all about that, having had it done to me a few hundred times.

Cathy tried to help Andy gain a clearer understanding of the sounds of individual letters and common letter combinations (*-tion, ph, -able, -tious*). They used commercially prepared phonics cards for the Orton-Gillingham approach from *Alphabetic Phonics* by Aylett Cox. For the sounds that gave Andy a great deal of trouble, he made his own cards. On the back of each card he drew a picture to remind him of the sound of the letter or letters. For example, on one card he printed *wr* and on the reverse side he drew a picture of someone writing. Every day he looked at the cards, said the names of the letters, the key words he had selected, and the accompanying sounds. He then wrote the letters on notebook paper, on the table top using his finger, or on a chalkboard. Sometimes Cathy said the sounds and Andy gave her the names of the letters orally. Then he visualized the letters as he said the sounds back. We referred to this activity as The Drill, though some of the students had other more humorous—and unprintable—names for it.

Gradually, Cathy began to teach syllable division rules to prove to Andy that large words were not impossible to read. They were just small words put together (*won/der/ful*). The first rule she taught him was the One-one-one Rule, which says that if a word has one syllable with one vowel and one letter after the vowel, the vowel sound is usually short (*hat*). A rule that was more complicated stated that when you have two consonants between two vowels, you divide the syllable between the two consonants (*cat/nip*). Andy wrote each of these in his notebook with examples to illustrate the rule. The discovery approach seemed to work well with Andy, which meant Cathy did not simply give him a rule. Instead, she showed him several examples and helped him discover for himself the rule governing the examples. Students remember something much better when they do most of the thinking.

Cathy also introduced Andy to spelling rules. Using the discovery approach again, she gave him a list of words ending in double consonants such as kiss, muff, pill, buzz. Andy quickly realized that *f, l, s,* and *z* were doubled when they were at the end of a one-syllable word. Cathy told him we call that the Floss Rule to help us remember it. That was Andy's first of many mnemonic devices designed to improve his memory.

Getting Andy to write was difficult. He was somewhat willing to attempt to read, but he drew the line at writing. An audible groan came forth whenever he was asked to write. The Orton-Gillingham philosophy of having a student read what is spelled, spell what is read, and practice handwriting with the same material seemed to be appropriate for Andy. Since he dreaded writing, there was no new information involved when he was asked to write, and this definitely seemed to help. The repetition was also good for him.

Shortly before it was time for spring break, Cathy told me her husband had been transferred to another state and they were moving soon. I was concerned about giving Andy another tutor because he had already had so much difficulty adjusting to Cathy. I had talked with Andy on numerous occasions, and we seemed to get along well together. After looking at my already crowded schedule, I decided to ask Andy if he would be willing to work with me.

I did not say, "Would you *like* to work with me?"

After spring break, Andy and I began meeting on a regular basis. I found him delightful. Our sessions together were full of teasing. When he read "tired" as "tried," I usually laughed and remarked, "There goes your dyslexia again!" Sometimes when I arrived a few minutes late, Andy would smile and say, "Oh, nuts, I thought you were in a meeting and wouldn't be able to get here!" We had a good, easy relationship. Andy didn't seem to be uncomfortable making mistakes in my presence. He had seen me make so many myself, he certainly shouldn't have been embarrassed.

Andy's writing improved, but not as much as his reading skills. Once I was giving him some dictation, and he made a lower case *t* when it should have been upper case. I mentioned the error and Andy grinned, "That's an informal *t*." Andy's refreshing sense of humor made working with him a joy.

I remember reading once that Hans Christian Andersen was able to live with his dyslexia and homely appearance because he had learned to laugh on a regular basis. How much healthier this is than to spend hours trying to find ways to hide problems with dyslexia from friends and relatives.

One day I asked Andy how he liked college. He readily told me he liked it more than high school because he had more freedom. He found it helpful to be able to select the professors he wanted rather than have his schedule planned for him as it was in high school. Like many other students, he liked the independence that came from being away from home.

I asked Andy about his new friends in college. Andy looked at me quickly and then glanced out the window. "I still feel like a loner sometimes," he confessed. "I have a few friends, but I feel different from other people. Sometimes I think I'm left out of things because the other guys know I'm different. On the other hand, I'm left out of some things because I have to spend so much time being tutored, and then I have to study longer than my friends do. That doesn't leave me a lot of free time."

Andy scratched his head and thought a minute. "Several times I've been on trips where I've met people I've really liked. When we try to exchange addresses, I'm always embarrassed. I usually solve the problem by telling them to write down my address and write to me."

"Andy, do most of your friends know you have dyslexia?"

"My good friends know, but not my casual friends. That is not a good opener. You don't just walk up to friends and say, 'Hey, you guys, I've got dyslexia! Guess what? I can't read!' No, that is definitely not a good opener."

When I began working with Andy, we continued The Drill, although he found it distasteful. Andy admitted, rather grudgingly, that it did help a lot. I think it helped him more than any other remediation exercises.

We also needed to work on reading from left to right. Sometimes Andy put the eraser end of a pencil under the words as he read them, gradually moving from left to right. At other times, Andy used a pencil to underscore a line as he read. When he reached the end of the line, the pencil backtracked and dropped to the beginning of the next line. Again he was to draw a line underneath the row of words. Putting his hand under the words and moving it to the right improved the accuracy of his reading. I believe the body contact with the page helped, too.

Before writing, Andy said the sentence aloud, which seemed to decrease the number of words he inserted or omitted when he tried to write a sentence before he said it. Many dyslexic writers seem to spend as much time erasing words as writing them. When Andy didn't know how to spell a word, I supplied it instantly. I made a note of the word so we could study it later. If we had stopped for each word he couldn't spell, he would have lost his train of thought.

After three years, Andy was able to read his textbooks. A huge victory. However, he tired easily. His tutor in coursework often read part of a paragraph and then Andy read the rest. They stopped frequently to discuss the content of what they had read. Andy high-lighted the main and supporting ideas and outlined the chapter in his notebook. For tests, he put the crucial information on index cards, which he carried with him and studied whenever he could. The key terms highlighted on the cards meant a net decrease in the amount of material he had to read. Mnemonic devices also helped Andy to memorize lists. He learned that mnemonic devices should be as silly as possible so he would remember them. The devices needed to contain something that would help him relate them to the list in specific ways.

Most of Andy's professors were very understanding about his problem with dyslexia. He was so verbal in class that his professors knew he understood the material. Andy's excellent verbal skills saved the day many times. Once I called a professor to make plans for an oral examination for Andy. The professor was surprised and said, "Are you sure we're talking about the same person? Are you calling me about Andy Anderson? He's one of the most outstand-ing students in my class. I find it hard to believe he needs an oral examination." I explained that Andy's strength was his verbal abil-ity, which was how he coped with his language problem. Andy's disability involved the written word only.

Andy was a junior before he attempted to take an English class. I was very apprehensive about his taking English in particu-lar. First, Andy's writing skills were still in the formative stages — negative comments from an English professor could do a great deal of harm. Second, the Rehabilitation Act Section 504 states that a handicapped student has a right to be tested in a manner that will indicate what the student knows, rather than to show up his handicap — unless the handicap itself is the area being tested. There is still some disagreement about how this affects English classes. The handicapped person certainly has a right to a time extension on tests, but does the student have the right to dictate themes, for example? Andy wouldn't need to dictate material, but he would need to have some guidance (and encouragement) as he wrote. I felt it was very risky for him to enroll in an English class on campus.

An alternative was to enroll Andy in the same class through a university with a correspondence program. We decided to do this, and his tutor guided him through assignments. Andy did all of the writing, and we didn't have to worry that an unintentional negative comment might delay his progress. He actually did much more writing than he would have in a class on campus. Andy learned a tremendous amount about English and enjoyed the switch from sitting in a classroom to taking a correspondence course.

When it was nearly time for Andy to graduate, I asked him to write a paper about reading and the problems he had experienced. Here is part of what he wrote:

How Reading Changed My Life

Reading is a necessity. If you cannot read, it hinders every thing in your life. I am more confident around my peers now because I can read. This makes me enjoy being around my peers more. I can read a menu in a restaurant as well as road signs. This was very embarrassing for me when I couldn't read. Sometimes I enjoy reading a magazine.

Life is more enjoyable and it is certainly less stressful now. The future is a lot brighter for me now that I know how to read.

When Andy went to the grocery store for the first time after moving out of the dormitory and into an apartment, he thought he had enough cash to pay for the items, but he didn't. He had to write a check. Quickly he looked at the cashier's name tag to get the name of the store. He knew how to spell the month but he couldn't spell the words indicating twenty-three dollars and forty-seven cents. He just wrote $23.47 on both lines and hoped no one would notice.

Andy saw me the next morning and said, "I have never been

so embarrassed in my life. I was so nervous I broke out in a sweat like I'd been running for miles. I could feel my heart beating and my hands shaking. I was desperate. I had completed two years of college and I couldn't spell my numbers. I'm tired of having to carry around cash all the time. Anyway, sometimes I have to be able to spell numbers on checks."

I thought for a moment, and then, recalling an idea from a classmate, I suggested, "Andy, suppose I type all of the numbers and reduce them on the copier. We can cover it with clear contact paper and you can attach it to your checkbook. That way you'll always be able to spell the numbers." Andy looked so relieved I felt I had handed him the moon and the stars.

A week later Andy came to see me with a broad grin on his face. "I just have to tell you this! I went to the grocery store again and I wrote a check. With the numbers there right above my blank check, I didn't have any trouble with filling out the check. What a relief! After that I went to the telephone company to pay the bill. I went up to the window and wrote my check right there where everyone could see. Because of my number list, I could write a check like anyone else. This is the best thing that's happened to me in ages! Thanks."

During Andy's first two years of college, he made nothing below a C, including many B's. He took difficult courses, such as Introduction to Biology, General Psychology, and World History, and he enrolled in none of the courses that were reported to be easy. His last two years of college included more classes in his major, Business Management, many of which were quite difficult. Calculus, Finance, and Accounting can be extremely difficult classes for any student, but Andy never gave up. He worked doggedly on assignments, never failing to ask for help when he really needed it. All of his professors were very complimentary of him, stating that he worked hard, always attended class, contributed to class discussions regularly, and seemed to understand the material.

Andy

Andy helped himself by not abusing his independence. Some students find their way to a local college hangout every night. Andy knew he had to study every night if he wanted to be successful in college. Many students have to learn the hard way that in college you don't get anything you don't work for. Cutting class, for example, is not a criminal offense. But it does mean you won't know what was taught during that class. Asking a fellow student for information about the missed class usually evokes only, "Ah, let's see, oh yes, we didn't do anything. The professor just talked." A price will be paid at exam time. Andy seemed to understand from the beginning. He was willing to work harder than his peers. And do it every day, not just occasionally.

Andy completed the requirements for his Bachelor's degree several years ago. He deserves an award for overcoming so many obstacles. But Andy doesn't need an award to know how far he has come. He succeeded in the pursuit of his Bachelor's degree and knows he can be successful at whatever is important to him. Certainly his future looks much brighter than a few years ago. He has learned to read books and magazines. He can read and write letters. His self-esteem has improved immeasurably.

Andy always wanted to work for his father's large company. Now, instead of believing he should have the most menial position, he knows he can make a real contribution to the company. True, Andy's spelling will probably never be "average," but he has learned how to use a dictionary, a computerized speller, and a word processing program with a spelling checker. When he needs to write a memorandum, he can use all of these. Still, it will be important for Andy to have a secretary who knows about his problems with dyslexia and what helps. For example, long reports should be read to him and important sections highlighted since reading will probably always be a tiring experience for Andy. After all, his dyslexia isn't going anywhere.

Andy has spoken at national and state conferences. He shared with teachers, psychologists, parents, and students his many traumatic experiences with dyslexia. He has spoken to graduate and undergraduate classes of future teachers and openly discussed his life as a dyslexic. He visited junior and senior high schools and spoke to students with learning disabilities there who were trying to decide if they should attend college. Some were trying to decide if they should continue to put forth any more effort at all in school since it seemed to them a hopeless situation. Andy easily communicated with these desperate young people. These teaching experiences were good for Andy, too. The more he shared his dyslexic experiences, the more he accepted and even appreciated his potential.

Andy began college as a functional nonreader and, within three years, learned to read his textbooks. He was never on probation in college, and he made the Dean's List twice. He developed excellent work habits, superb social skills, and a determination to do well. He has a lot to be proud of.

Since Andy's graduation from college he has been promoted three times in the family company. He has been the sole administrator in two states, and he has been very successful. His employees like him both as a manager and as a friend.

Andy, I take my hat off to you. Throughout your life you worked much harder than your peers. Now you are a professional in business, and now you have the edge.

chapter 5

eric

ERIC RARELY READ his textbooks. Instead, as he worked on his chemistry major and political science minor in college, he listened for phrases from his professors that would indicate what might be on the tests. Phrases typical of those that attracted Eric's attention were, "one might suggest," "another important point," and "in conclusion." When he wrote his examination answers, Eric frequently used such phrases and also tried to echo the words he had heard the professors speak in class. He found that professors would note things in the margins of his papers such as, "very good sentence."

At that point in his education, Eric gave little thought to why he studied differently from his peers. He was then telling himself, "I'm mentally retarded, but if I work extra hard, no one will notice." At the same time he found ways to hide his difficulties with reading from his teachers and classmates. To compensate for not reading the textbooks Eric listened more intently in class, dove into class discussions and memorized his professors' favorite phrases for use during test taking.

Given his reading problem, Eric instinctively knew that he had to maximize his classroom learning—or else suffer the consequences of failing grades.

During his college days Eric became known as a wheeler-dealer. "I got involved in business deals where a knack for selling was required," he told me. "I also had a knack for repairing things, such as washing machines and chairs; so I watched the classifieds for bargains, bought, repaired or refinished items, and made money selling them. Once I bought a broken-down motorcycle for a song and overhauled it. I had never even ridden a motorcycle before, but I was able to put that cycle back together and sell it for a tidy profit."

Eric's endless supply of energy allowed him to engage in such business deals and still spend more time studying than his peers. He realized that earning money was no substitute for getting his schoolwork done. Eric's main problems came in grammar, punctuation, and spelling, with spelling being "creative" at best. He put great effort, however, into choosing words for essay answers from among those he knew how to spell, but nonetheless still made ridiculous errors. However, Eric's verbal skills usually more than compensated for his problems with reading and written language. He graduated from college with honors. His grade-point average was 3.84 on a four-point scale. His goal was to obtain an M.D. and become a surgeon.

Eric's scores on the Medical College Admissions Test (MCAT) were low, and, not surprisingly, his reading score was the lowest of all. In spite of his MCAT scores, Eric navigated the admissions process well. Medical school professors who interviewed him were impressed with his articulate speech, and he was admitted to the School of Medicine at Marshall University in Huntington, West Virginia.

The first year of medical studies was a shock for Eric. He managed a C average the fall semester but fell off into low C's and D's in the spring. He was summoned to meet with the Dean.

The Dean asked Eric if he was working too much on the side. Eric replied that no, he was actually studying all the time. In fact, he said, he'd never worked so hard at school in all his life. Finally, Eric looked at the Dean with a discouraged expression and confessed, "The truth is I don't read well enough to read textbooks of a thousand pages or more." The Dean asked Eric if he ever read for pleasure. "No," Eric said, "and what's more, I never had to read textbooks until this year."

"I remember what I hear in the lectures," he told the Dean, "but everything that's on the test is not presented in lectures."

Following that meeting the Dean picked up the telephone and called my office.

"Dr. Guyer, I have a young man here who isn't doing well in class," he told me after briefly introducing himself as the Dean of the Medical School. "It seems he's working as diligently as possible. I'm sure he's intelligent and I suspect the problem may be dyslexia. I wonder if you could test him?"

A few days later my secretary ushered into my office a handsome young man with black wavy hair wearing a small gold chain around his neck. He was warm and effusive, one of those rare people you feel as if you've always known even though you're just meeting for the first time. While Eric was with me, I noticed that my female graduate assistants suddenly had more occasions than usual to stop by my office and ask for direction or see if there was anything they could do for me.

Before testing Eric, I asked him about his life before medical school. Perhaps there were signs in earlier years that would explain his failure as a freshman med student.

I learned that Eric's father had been an exceptionally fine student. After marriage, he completed his bachelor's degree and attended law school on the GI Bill. An avid reader who found school stimulating, he went on to earn a Master's in English at evening school and eventually even completed all the course requirements for his doctorate.

Eric's mother, meanwhile, had put her energy into raising her sons. Eric was the fourth of five. The oldest brother was an attorney; another had earned a Ph.D. and another an M.A. in Engineering. Only Eric's youngest brother had had difficulty in school. He joined the Marines upon graduation from high school and was happier in the Corps than he had ever been in school. That brother was now working on a degree in Criminal Justice, though, according to Eric, he rarely read and spent most of his time in outdoor recreation.

I then asked Eric about himself.

"Well," he sighed, "it wasn't possible to avoid school entirely, so I went. But I didn't like going to school. I remember being a group leader in kindergarten and I did pretty well. But, for some reason I wasn't interested in reading or learning letters and writing. My older brothers were all into that stuff, but not me; I liked to run around and do things. I always had lots of energy. Another thing, I remember that I stuttered until I was in the second grade, then the stuttering just disappeared."

Eric averred that he probably was an "average student" until fifth grade. It was at that point that a teacher changed his attitude toward schoolwork. The teacher's name was Dewey Parr.

"Mr. Parr thought I was a gifted student even though I made only average grades," Eric recalled warmly. "Mr. Parr had a radio station in his room for students to report about school and community happenings. One day he told me that if I got all my work for him done correctly the first half of the week, I could work on the radio station the whole second half.

"For the first time in my life I actually got excited about school. I worked hard on my assignments. Eventually, I became the head disc jockey on Mr. Parr's station. That made me look good to my friends. Then a local radio station invited me on the air to talk about the station we had in the elementary school. My picture landed in the newspaper. Wow! It was exciting."

Because of Dewey Parr, Eric began to feel very good about himself, even began to regard himself as a leader. His grades improved as well. Soon he made Honor Roll for the first time. Eric's grades continued their upward course until he had become a straight-A student.

"I don't think Mr. Parr was always understood by the other teachers," Eric commented. "He was so ahead of his time. He made learning so much fun I could hardly wait to get to school each morning and I didn't want to go home in the afternoon. Isn't that what good teachers are about? In that fifth-grade year with him I learned more than I'd learned in the previous five years put together. He was the best teacher I've ever had, before or since. I still send him a Christmas card every year."

In high school Eric made a B in only three classes; in all the others he received an A. He was class president in grades seven, ten, and eleven; student body president in grades nine and twelve, and salutatorian at graduation. Eric always had a high level of energy. He was all-state in baseball and also lettered as a running back in football, wrestling, and track and field. He also performed in several high-school musicals.

To achieve all this Eric arrived at school early, faithfully attended classes and paid keen attention, took part in competitive sports after school, and still had energy to spare. When in the cast of a musical production, he often did not return home until ten or eleven at night. Channeling his excessive energy into positive activities was certainly one key to Eric's success — in school and in his social life.

Nonetheless, Eric told me, "Dr. G, I know I looked like an outstanding student with zero academic problems. But believe me, I hated to read and my spelling was atrocious. When all my memorization techniques weren't enough and I actually had to read part of a book, I'd read a chapter four or five times before I understood anything I read. I never said anything to anybody, but deep down inside, I knew there was something wrong with me."

Eric scored poorly on the ACT and SAT tests for admission to college. His high school guidance counselor was so concerned he had Eric work with an educational counselor. That counselor ended up telling Eric and his family that, in all probability, Eric would not do well in college. A small voice inside Eric began to whisper to him that he really wasn't very smart. Otherwise, why couldn't he do well on the national tests? Eric finally decided his success in high school came because he worked harder than the other students and because his teachers liked him. Eric had always made an effort to see that everyone he met liked him.

Drawing upon many of the same techniques that had seen him through high school, Eric managed to negotiate impressive grades during his college career, as I've already described. He met his Waterloo, however, in first year medical school. And, had it not been for that call to me from the Dean, it is doubtful Eric would have been able to complete his M.D. He was in all likelihood heading for a washout.

I proceeded in my analysis of Eric by putting him through an intelligence test. In the midst of testing, when he came upon an especially difficult question he often grinned as he answered it and said something like, "Dr. G, want to know how I know this answer? Dr. Johnson mentioned this in my sophomore calculus class and I've never forgotten it." Not only did Eric uncannily recall bits of information, he also remembered when and where he had first picked them up. Of the many people I have tested, Eric has thus far been the only person able to do that.

When I scored Eric's intelligence test I was surprised to discover he had an IQ of 150. This placed him in the top one-half of one percent of the U.S. population. I had rarely worked with anyone this bright. An IQ of 140 is the beginning of genius.

The achievement testing went differently. Here Eric definitely did not rank in the top echelons. I gave Eric a variety of tests to evaluate reading, spelling, written language, mathematics, and critical analytical skills. After listening to him recount his past, it did not surprise me that this medical student scored at the tenth-grade level in reading and spelling. Although Eric's oral language was very good, even exceptional, his written language was on a more elementary level. Partly, this was because he limited himself to words he thought he knew how to spell. Only his mathematical and analytical skills were on the appropriate grade level for his years of education.

Eric's tests indicated a diagnosis of dyslexia. In the recommendations section of my report to the Dean, I prescribed the following:

1) Eric should take a reduced load of basic science classes so he will not be overwhelmed with reading material. However, during the clinical years of medical school, he should be able to cope with the normal course load.
2) He should be given time extensions on all tests and take them in a separate room to avoid distractions [This has been made possible by Section 504 of the Rehabilitation Act of 1973].
3) He should attend Summer Medical H.E.L.P. [a remedial program for dyslexic medical students that I was in the process of organizing at Marshall University] and
4) Eric should order Textbooks on Tape from Recordings for the Blind in Princeton, New Jersey, so he can listen to his textbooks as he reads.

A few days later I ran into Eric on campus. We stopped for a few minutes to chat. I brought up his unusually high score on the IQ tests. He looked at me intently, then murmured, "I thought I was mentally retarded. I've known all my life I was different. Something was wrong with me that kept me from wanting to read. But I'm an optimist, and I found I could make up for being 'dumb' by being persistent. And it worked—until I got into medical school. I was so afraid when you tested me. But now I just thank God that my mind and my brain are okay. And I have you to thank, too, Dr. Guyer, for finding that out for me."

Eric then put his arms around me and gave me a big hug. As he strolled off, I did not move for a moment. I felt so much happiness for Eric. But there was another feeling mixed in, I could tell. I identified it as a great sadness over the numbers of people who go through life thinking they are retarded when, in truth, they are beset by learning disabilities that they do not understand.

It seems almost incomprehensible that a young man with an IQ of 150 could spend years thinking of himself as retarded. How many others are out there thinking that of themselves? What kind of lives are they leading?

When the time came for a meeting with the Associate Dean, there was a strained silence in the room. Eric, his father, and I all sat there nervously knowing that Eric's continued enrollment in medical school depended upon the Associate Dean's assent.

The Associate Dean asked me to explain my diagnosis of dyslexia and discuss Eric's chances for succeeding in medical school. I brought up Eric's exceedingly high scores on the intelligence test and Eric's father chimed in by saying how surprised he was that his son had scored so high in IQ. The Associate Dean looked at him a moment, then said, "If Eric weren't such a gifted person, I doubt we would even be having this meeting."

After going over test scores and the characteristics of dyslexia, I mentioned the research of Gallaburda and Geschwind on the advantages of being dyslexic. This research indicates that many dyslexics enjoy exceptional right-brain skills, such as well-developed verbal abilities, athleticism, mathematics skills, and also keen understanding of other people and their problems. I pointed out that Eric seemed to possess all of these gifts. He certainly was creative, verbal, compassionate, athletic, and good in mathematics. I also emphasized that it would be necessary for Eric to continue to concentrate on his gifts while simultaneously attempting to correct his deficiencies.

Thankfully, our presentation won over the Associate Dean. He agreed that Eric should take a slightly reduced course load in the fall and have time extensions on all tests, which would be administered to him in a separate room away from his classmates. Eric was to remediate any necessary classes during the summer months.

If Eric's Dean had not been so perceptive and so open to hearing from a professional in LD education, Eric would by now probably be a former medical student, possibly depressed and frustrated and convinced that he was an incompetent. Failure has profound effects on people, especially upon individuals who are sensitive and discerning. Eric might well have been scarred for life. Thank God for a Dean who was not fixated on lack of ability and laziness as the only possible explanations for academic failure.

When Summer Medical H.E.L.P. began, Eric and three other students with learning problems came daily for assistance in study skills, note- and test-taking strategies, and remedial reading with emphasis on comprehension. Since all of the students were dyslexic, my staff and I used some of the many adaptations of the Orton-Gillingham approach.

We learned that none of the students in our program possessed good study skills. They all tried to study for eight or ten hours at a stretch. Their method was to read and re-read the material. As dyslexics, they wasted hours of time in daydreaming or nodding off. We encouraged them to use a timer and study for no more than one hour at a time. We also prescribed a ten- to fifteen-minute break each hour, and exercise during the break. When the weather was bad they could run up and down the steps inside their building. Occasionally, they were to break for a nutritious snack.

Their note-taking skills were poor, too, to say the least. So we taught them the Kesselman-Turkel and Peterson technique called t-notes. With this method, the student outlines a chapter in the middle section of a page before going to class. During the lecture the student writes in the right column what the professor emphasizes from the textbook and jots down any new material not in the text. The student puts key words in the left column. These key terms help students focus on what's important. Students can also quiz themselves by looking at the key words and checking to see if they understand their significance.

We also taught the students techniques for improving their test-taking. We showed them, for example, how not to fall into the traps of multiple choice tests. (These pitfalls include reading negative statements as positive, omitting key words such as "but," "never," and "occasionally." Another frequent error is reading into a question information that isn't there.) We discussed the importance of underlining key words in test questions in order to appreciate the heart of the question. Most of our students had also been mis-reading positive statements as negatives, and vice-versa. If, however, they underlined words such as "never," "not," and "always," they were more likely to understand the questions correctly.

We also tested these students to assess their skills in "attacking" the spelling and pronunciation of words. When students did not know how to spell or pronounce certain letter combinations correctly (such as *-tion* or *spl-*), we showed them how, making it clear that we were attempting to fill in the missing pieces of mortar in their "house of language." Eric and his fellow medical students also progressed through a series of remedial reading and reading comprehension exercises.

Eric began his second year of medical school the last week of August. He had been carefully tutored on how to study, how long to study, how to take different types of tests, and how to monitor his attention span. The Associate Dean had accepted my request for exceptions in testing for Eric and conveyed the arrangements to Eric's professors. Everything seemed to be in place.

But there were hitches. Eric's classmates were rather vocal in their criticism of his receiving time extensions on tests. They made it clear that they felt such privileged treatment for one student was unfair. And one professor told Eric he felt Eric was using his learning problem "as a crutch." Another professor said that while he would go along with the special arrangements for test taking, he thought it dishonest for Eric to have more time than his peers to finish a test.

These professors and students, of course, had never examined the literature on the effect of time extensions on normally achieving students and on students with learning disabilities. Normally achieving students did not attain significantly higher scores with a time extension, while LD students in fact did. Furthermore, there was no significant difference in achievement between the two groups when the learning disabled students were granted time extensions. These time extensions helped to level the playing field for LD students.

The second year of medical school, even with all the helps we had organized, was not easy for Eric. He maintained a high C average, which kept him out of trouble with the Academic Standards Committee, but he was frustrated because he wanted desperately to do much better. The better, though, would come later. Even at that stage, he knew he could look forward to the later years of medical school, because there would be much less required reading than in the first years.

After Eric completed his basic science courses, he was required to take the first part of the National Board of Medical Examiners. This test lasts all day for two days straight. With a time extension, the test took Eric nearly three days to complete and left him mentally and physically exhausted. Reading always wore Eric out. With the time extension at least, he could allow himself to concentrate on what he was reading instead of worrying about the time left to finish.

Eric agonized through the six-week period it took to return his score. One of his professors stopped me on campus one sultry afternoon during that period and told me, "Eric doesn't have a chance in hell of passing that examination." I only smiled and said, "He just may surprise you." A score of 380 was required for passing. When the results came in, Eric had achieved 550 on some of the sub-tests and an overall score of 500.

Everyone in the medical school talked about Eric's success, and he was never the same after those scores. That achievement greatly bolstered his confidence. Eric became determined that he was going to be a physician—and a good one.

The third year of medical school began with an unpleasant experience. A clinical professor approached Eric after he had corrected the first test and said, "Eric, I understand that you are dyslexic. Dyslexics are known as cheaters. Did you cheat on my test?" At first Eric thought the man was joking, but the professor did not smile. Later, Eric told me he wanted to scream at that professor, "Is that like all football players are dumb?" Eric was so angry and hurt he couldn't concentrate on his courses for the remainder of the week.

After that initial negative experience, Eric progressed smoothly through the third and fourth years of medical school. He excelled in hands-on learning. When he was required to make presentations in front of his peers, professors, and staff physicians, he used his superb communication skills to good advantage. Unlike most of his peers, Eric enjoyed speaking in public, and it certainly made a difference in his grades. He found that most of his friends would rather study textbooks than talk to patients or be questioned verbally by clinical professors. Oral language was the medium that had always allowed Eric to compensate for his reading and spelling problems, and he began to excel as a medical student. In his third year of medical school Eric received three B's and the rest A's. During his fourth year he received all A's.

Eric had always been very good in sports and his visual-motor integration skills were well-developed. It was not surprising to me therefore that the rotations in surgery gave Eric great joy.

Fourth-year medical students are encouraged to select the area of specialty that appeals to them and to take their off-campus rotations in locations where they hope to go for a residency. Eric became quite interested in plastic and reconstructive surgery and selected a medical center in the Midwest for one of his rotations. His interest in this sub-specialty of surgery blossomed, and he performed phenomenally well in the operating room. He also continued to exhibit an exceptional ability to communicate with patients and their families. In fact, Eric could have meaningful conversations with almost anyone without making them feel threatened. If Eric couldn't communicate with someone, chances are something was dreadfully wrong with that person.

When it was time for residencies, Eric applied to the medical center where he had done a rotation in plastic and reconstructive surgery. No one there had been aware of his learning problems when he was doing his rotation. But this time, when he went for the interview with the department chairman, he knew the Dean's letter had included information stating he was a dyslexic. The "Dean's letter" is essentially an assessment and recommendation of a medical student by the Dean or a member of the Dean's staff. This letter, based on grades and faculty comments, is an important part of the student's application for residency. The Dean acknowledged that Eric had dyslexia, but he also stated that Eric had learned how to deal with his problem. At the Dean's request I also wrote a letter stating that dyslexia would not interfere with Eric's ability to function successfully as a physician. I was delighted to be able to do this for Eric, because I felt if anyone could compensate for problems with dyslexia, it was Eric. When Eric sat for the interview with the chairman of the department, he had a sense that everything went very well.

Several months later, Eric answered his phone and heard a voice say, "Dr. Li would like to speak with you. Please hold."

Dr. Li, he remembered, was chairman of the Department of Surgery at the Big Ten university where Eric hoped to be invited to do his residency.

"Hello, Eric?"

"Yes."

"This is Dr. Li. Perhaps you remember me. I interviewed you a few months ago about—"

"Yes, Dr. Li. I remember you very well. How are you, sir?"

"Fine. Yes, just fine, thank you. I hope you're the same."

"Yes, sir."

There was a pause.

"Oh, God," Eric thought, "he called to give me the bad news. He hopes I'm fine, too, so I can take it. We don't have to have bad feelings here. We're both fine."

"Eric," Dr. Li rejoined, "you probably know we get a lot of

applicants every year and we couldn't possibly accept them all. So we choose very selectively. Do you have any idea how many applicants we had for next term?"

"No, sir, not really."

"Well, we had more than twelve hundred. And do you know how many openings we have in our department?"

By now Eric was in anguish. Was he being asked questions to which he should know the answers? Weren't the interviews over months ago? With his doubts and his hopes both strong and competing with each other, Eric said, "No, sir, I don't."

"Well, Eric, we have six positions. Exactly six. And we have twelve hundred applicants. And do you know why we selected you?"

There followed another pause, this time created by Eric, who had taken the phone away from his ear and was looking at the tiny holes in the receiver to see if the instrument was playing tricks on him.

"I'm sorry, Dr. Li. What did you just say?"

"I said we selected you to join us for your residency, but I wonder if you know why we picked you."

Though instantly euphoric, Eric still could say only, "No, sir, not really."

"We selected you because you're unique. Straight-A medical graduates aren't that hard to find. We've learned that straight-A students don't always make the best physicians. On the other hand, you had a problem, and you worked to overcome it with everything that's in you. You could have given up but you didn't. It must have been very painful to have a few professors say you were dishonest when you asked for exceptions in testing. I know that some professors said you would never make it, but you didn't quit. You're persistent, Eric. And that's why we selected you. You're a survivor. We believe you're the type of person who will make an exceptionally good reconstructive surgeon. I look forward to working with you."

Eric put down the telephone and heaved a long, happy sigh. He knew it! He knew if he just stuck in there and refused to give up, if he worked as hard as he knew how, if he put his all into it, he would overcome. This had to be the happiest day of his life.

Shortly after he received the telephone call, Eric was in my office. When I saw the expression on his face, I knew immediately he had good news.

"Dr. G, I got a call today from the chairman of surgery for my first choice in residency. He said twelve hundred people applied for just six positions. Just six! I couldn't believe it, Dr. G, when he told me that they selected me. He said straight-A students were a dime a dozen. He was looking for someone who had problems in life but had been able to cope with them, like me with dyslexia. He said those are the kind of people who make good doctors. And he wanted someone who knew how to communicate with people, not just operate on them. You know, Dr. G, I've spent all my life wanting to be like everyone else, and now I get the one thing I've wanted more than anything in the world because I'm different! Life can be beautiful."

Eric gave me a big hug before he left my office. I kept my smile for the rest of the day.

When Eric received his M.D. degree, I was there beaming as if he were my own son. Eric taught me about never giving up, about looking at the bright side when things get tough. For my part, I helped Eric discover his unusual degree of intelligence, a blessing he can use to ease human suffering. I taught him how to compensate for his learning deficiencies. Most of all, I was able to help him see that dyslexia can be a gift of greatness rather than a handicapping condition.

Eric's residency in plastic and reconstructive surgery was exceptional from the beginning. I keep a copy of an evaluation Eric's father sent me from unusually complimentary professors. Each area has checks in the column marked "outstanding," but the comments at the bottom were what caught my eye. One professor wrote, "Eric has an uncanny ability to communicate with patients and their families. I have been told many times and have seen for myself how Eric goes out of his way to explain everything. He never seems to mind repeating information over and over in a pleasant way." Another professor scrawled, "Eric is an outstanding surgeon who improves each year. Like fine wine, he will get even better!" I can't help feeling proud each time I read that, knowing I am in a small way responsible for this unique young man's becoming a physician.

How different Eric's life could have been. He might have attended a medical school which simply dismissed students not maintaining the required grade-point average. Fortunately for Eric and probably for all of us, someone wanted to find out why a student was failing. Because of a highly professional and observant Dean, Eric will not be a frustrated and hurt young man in search of a profession outside of his chosen field. Instead, he is becoming an outstanding surgeon who publishes papers in medical journals and presents papers at medical conferences.

Now Eric, with his 150 IQ, has been allowed the opportunity to add his contributions to those of other successful dyslexics in the field of medicine, luminaries such as Dr. Harvey Cushing, neurologist, Dr. Paul Ehrlich, bacteriologist, and Dr. William Osler, surgeon.

chapter 6

wanda

A BARRAGE OF phone calls followed the talk show I did that Friday morning on learning disorders. Most callers were concerned about their children. Now at four o'clock, while I was saying to myself, "No, I can't talk to anyone else," my secretary asked, "Can you take one more call?"

From the other end of the line came... silence. I repeated my greeting. "May I help you?" Silence. But I could tell someone was there. I insisted again, "Hello? May I help you?"

"What should I do...?" a timid female voice queried. "I think I'm retarded."

This didn't sound quite like the hopelessness I had heard so often that day in parents' voices.

"Why do you think you're retarded?"

"I'm thirty-three years old and I can't read anything—not even the comics. I heard your radio program this morning in my car. I remembered your phone number and decided to call you."

"Did you write the number down?"

"No, I just remembered it."

That didn't sound retarded to me. I asked the caller her name and her neighborhood. She said she was Wanda Black and told me she lived in one of the most exclusive areas of town. A retarded lady from the country club set? Intriguing.

So I made an appointment to meet Wanda Black.

Over the weekend I couldn't help but think of Wanda. I wondered what her life in upper-middle-class America must be like if she couldn't read, "not even the comics." Beyond that curiosity I felt a sense of alarm. She had sounded sincerely convinced that she was mentally retarded. Country club or just country, that kind of self-diagnosis would be hard to live with.

On Monday at 9:30 in the morning my secretary buzzed and said Wanda had arrived. I followed my usual custom of walking into the waiting room "on an errand" so as to get a glimpse of the new client. Doing so that morning I came upon an attractive, stylishly dressed young woman with auburn hair brushing her shoulders. Tasteful blue dress, complementing accessories, excellent posture—this was a person you would notice in a crowd. I glanced around. Who else might be waiting? But the young red-haired woman was alone in the room. I walked past her to my mailbox and retrieved something or nothing.

"Wanda Black?" I asked as I retraced my steps.

"Yes."

Tall and slender, she moved gracefully across the room and into my office. I looked into a pair of alert, inquisitive eyes and introduced myself. Retarded? If so, this was the most well-handled case of mental retardation I had ever seen. She took a chair awkwardly, hid trembling hands in her lap and began our session in a quavering voice. She volunteered that she had had difficulty finding a parking space near the university. She couldn't parallel park, she said, because she became confused when turning the steering wheel. "Do you have problems remembering the difference between left and right?" I asked.

"Oh, yes!" she said, like a person hungering for confession—and for help. "I always look at my wedding ring to figure out which way is left. Without the ring I could never know which way to go."

I made a note. Then I asked, "Wanda, why do you think you're mentally retarded?"

She tried to pull herself together, found her courage and said, "Because I can't read." Wanda hastened to explain herself: "Three years ago I decided to try one more time, so I had my ophthalmologist examine my eyes. Once again he told me I had no visual impairments. I remember looking at him with tears in my eyes and blurting out. 'Well, if my eyes are so good, why can't I read anything?' What he said next broke my heart: 'Not even the comics? I thought anybody could read the comics!' He told me my eyes were perfect but said maybe there was something wrong with my brain. He suggested I see a neurologist. That did it. I figured I must be retarded. Why go through the embarrassment of having a neurologist look into my obviously inferior brain? So I never went to see one."

Wanda had said about as much negative as any person could and still seek help.

"I am retarded." In other words, "I'm guilty of that." I invited her to take a walk with me around the university campus. She seemed relieved to leave her chair and get outside. I felt better, too, out in the fresh air, moving between sunlit spaces and shade. We small-talked until I felt Wanda was relaxed and feeling that she could trust me. When I asked if her husband knew she couldn't read when they wed, her face flushed.

"No," she murmured, "He didn't. I didn't tell him because I was afraid that if he knew, he'd stop respecting me. I loved him so much, I didn't want to lose him."

"I can't help wondering how you could have kept that from him, since you knew each other so well," I commented. "I mean, you were getting married—and he didn't know that you couldn't read? How could that be?"

"We were very much in love, or we wouldn't have gotten married. But I also knew that Jim himself was absolutely normal, I mean with no handicaps whatever, so I pretended to be normal too. I got away with it. Once in awhile, if Jim gave me something to read because, for instance, he thought it was funny, I pretended to read the article and chuckled occasionally. I looked for cues from him as to where I should laugh as my eyes moved down the lines. It worked."

"So you never told him? He still doesn't know?"

"Oh, no. I told him on our wedding night. I remember I was sitting on the bed, kinda nervous, and I just blurted it out. I felt like a volcano that had been holding back something big, something that just had to explode. After all, we were married now, and I had been very uncomfortable about lying to Jim. So I told him."

Wanda was smiling now. Somehow this was a good memory. A wedding night, some bad news slips out... Unless that news involved a major crime or sexual deviance, maybe a wedding night wasn't the worst time to disclose an unpleasant secret. I asked her how she put the news to Jim.

"Well," she said, "I just told him the truth. I said, 'Jim, I've tried to tell you this every day since we met, but it just wouldn't come out before. I couldn't seem to make myself tell you because I don't want you to think less of me."

An exceptionally kind and compassionate man, Jim sat down on the bed next to Wanda and put his arm around her. "Wanda, nothing you could tell me would make me love you less. What's so terrible that you can't tell me about it? Did you have a husband? A baby? An abortion? What?"

Wanda laughed nervously when Jim gave these examples. "Oh, no, no, no! Nothing like that," she told him, looking down at the hand that was clinging to both of hers. "It's worse!" Jim looked at her hard, wondering what could be worse than the things he'd mentioned.

"I can't read, Jim! I've never been able to read. I've tried as hard as I know how, but I never seem to be able to do it. I have to pretend and lie about it all the time. I don't ever want to lie to you anymore, so I'm telling you. You're the first one I've ever told."

For a moment Jim looked quite uncomfortable. He had anticipated something totally different, probably sexual in nature. Now he was more confused than upset. What Wanda was revealing to him was far afield from what he had braced himself to hear.

"But Wanda," he finally rejoined. "You always seemed so well informed about everything. How could you keep up without reading?"

Wanda sat still. She wanted to find the right words. She was still quite anxious about losing Jim's acceptance of her. Jim felt her uncertainty and held her closer.

"I'm like blind people, Jim; you know how people are always saying that they hear better 'cause they can't see? I listen better to everything because I can't read. I really listen hard—to people, to TV, to the radio, whatever… You know, I even watch Sesame Street hoping that it'll teach me to read. But nothing works. This is just the way I am."

Jim told his bride that her problem didn't matter to him. Of course, Jim could scarcely imagine then how greatly Wanda's "little problem" would affect her life, and the lives of everybody around her.

Jim and Wanda settled into married life. Wanda always kept a lovely home for Jim, but she developed her cooking skills with some difficulty since she could not get much help from recipes. Nevertheless, she told me that she did eventually become an excellent cook. I asked Wanda how she learned to cook when she couldn't read a recipe. "It was hard at first," she replied. "But I soon learned what general ingredients I'd need for this or that dish. I always got hold of recipes with pictures of the ingredients. If I can't figure out the necessary words, I ask Jim before he goes off to work. He never minds reading for me. He's really sweet. Along the way, though, I've had some flops. I guess I have made some of the world's funniest looking dishes!"

This reminded me of my first effort at making hot rolls as a new bride. They were so hard that one bounced right up off the floor when I accidentally dropped it. I boxed up one of those rolls and shipped it to my mother, two thousand miles away, so she could laugh along with my husband over my initiation into homemaking.

Wanda paused, pensive for a moment. "I think I just have a knack for cooking," she mused. "Everyone thinks of me as a good cook." Then she smiled in happy pride.

Wanda also told me a bit about her domestic life: "After we had been married for awhile, we began to have a few friends in. Sometimes we played games like Scrabble that meant you had to read. I always dreaded seeing that Scrabble box come out. I would just tell our guests that I didn't much like board games, so I'd fix snacks for everybody while they played. I'd make jokes such as, 'I'll get double and triple points from your stomachs instead of your words.' But when they all left, I'd suddenly feel really depressed, and then Jim was stuck with me."

Wanda told me more stories about her life married to a successful businessman. After our rather tense, tentative beginning, I discovered that Wanda had a charming personality and the ability to make others feel relaxed and even laugh. I noticed, however, that her jokes were often about herself. I wondered if that was healthy. I grew to see that Wanda essentially traded on her bubbly personality to mask her inner anxiety about being illiterate. That way no one would guess that she was dying a slow inner death—a suffocation of self-worth.

One day I took Wanda to a space I had been given for testing, in the basement the School of Education building on campus. It was typical for Special Education to be located in the basement, but I didn't object. It was very quiet down there and free from distractions. Which was ideal. I asked Wanda to sign her name. Her signature was perfectly formed. She could also write her address and the names of her children. She told me though that she really didn't know what she was writing. She had simply memorized the letters in their proper order for those specific words.

When I gave her an intelligence test, Wanda was too anxious to answer many items correctly. Later we would do a re-test when she was more relaxed. Achievement testing would have been a waste of time, for Wanda's reading vocabulary was limited to a

Richie

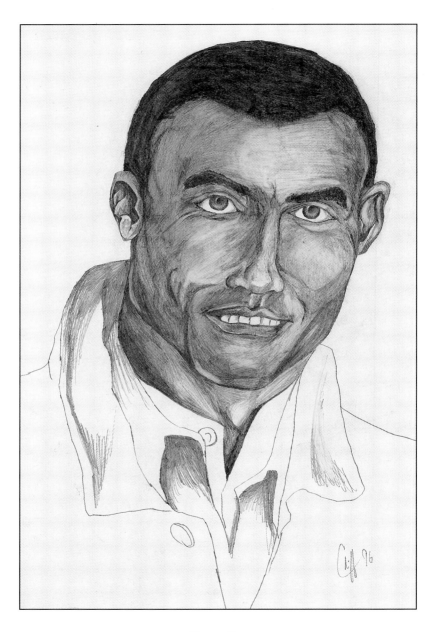

Cornelius

Andy

Eric

Dave

Craig

Wanda

Greta

handful of survival words such as *exit, enter, men, women.*

Wanda appeared exactly on time for her next appointment, looking as pretty and well-groomed as before. I wanted to know more about her school experience, so I asked, "Wanda, how did you get through public school without learning to read?"

"I had remedial reading in elementary school. It didn't help."

A long silence set in. Wanda seemed to be like a sky filling with storm clouds. My question had apparently shaken her up emotionally. Inadvertently, I had triggered a flood of hurtful memories and feelings from her school days. Over the years I have learned that so few of my LD students have good news to report from their past educational experiences.

Teachers, peers, and even family members often are ignorant of the difference between a learning disability and stupidity or retardation, and, out of that ignorance, they can say things that cause pain.

"When I told my remedial reading teacher that I couldn't tell the difference between *d* and *b* and some other letters, she just shrugged and said I would 'grow out of it, not to worry.' I'm still waiting."

Wanda was struggling with a great welling up of anger. She was scarred not only by her illiteracy but also by the thoughtlessness of others from her past. How deep were those scars? I wondered.

"The reversal problems are something you probably cannot outgrow by yourself," I told her. "You'll need help in learning another way to see those letters on a page." We continued to talk about school. Soon I learned that Wanda was usually scared of going there. This fear had begun in the first grade when she didn't learn to read while all her classmates did. After that, summer after summer, more and more, she dreaded the first week of September and the return to school. In bed during late August nights she had nightmares of being called on to read.

After a few weeks of dismal failure trying to get Wanda to read, teachers typically gave up on her and relegated her to the rear of the class.

Wanda recalled: "I remember one classmate trying to help me. We liked each other and so she thought she'd pitch in and help, throw me the ball, so to speak. Only she didn't know I couldn't catch it.

"'You don't know the *alphabet!*' I can still hear the tone in her voice. I never asked for help from a classmate again."

Though she didn't ask, occasionally when Wanda was called upon, children around her would whisper answers to her. But her best help came from her ability to read what she had heard the teachers say in class. "My ears were always busy," was the way she put it.

Fate spared Wanda the greater cruelties of school until the fifth grade. At that level a teacher insisted that Wanda march to the front of the class and read aloud. Being unprepared, this teacher told her, was no excuse.

Wanda's reading was scheduled for first thing on the morrow. She would have to read a random section of a passage that the teacher had assigned to the class. That evening at home Wanda tried hard to learn all the words in the passage, but there were too many. Facing horrible visions of humiliation, she couldn't get to sleep all night long.

Nothing Wanda imagined that night was as bad as what actually happened. As soon as the roll was called, the teacher told Wanda to go to the front and read from pages the teacher had selected. Wanda told the teacher, "I'm not ready, and I can't do it!"

"You come right here to me, young lady!" her teacher snapped. Her dark eyes blazed with determination. "Put your hands on this trash can." Wanda did as the teacher asked, and her teacher then whipped her with a switch in front of the entire class. Girls were rarely whipped, which doubled the embarrassment Wanda suffered that day.

"Now sit in the back row for the rest of this year, young lady!" the teacher hissed after the whipping. "People who don't care enough to try to learn don't deserve to sit with the rest of us."

Wanda hung her head as low as possible to hide bitter tears of humiliation. She sank down into the desk seat, her red curls tumbling around her face, and wished with all her might that a black hole would swallow her up.

"I wouldn't mind looking like a Mongoloid if I could just read," she told me later. "Everyone says I'm pretty. But I don't care what I look like. I just want to read."

Wanda's look of utter hopelessness was unforgettable to me. I felt anger toward the heartless fifth-grade teacher so blinded by her ignorance of learning disabilities. I had a strong desire to track her down and drag her to the steps of City Hall, where, before her incredulous eyes, I would burn her teaching certificate. Who gave a woman like this a license to teach children?

The next day none of her classmates had the courage to defend Wanda against the teacher. She never told anyone at home of the disgraceful scene she had endured because she was so ashamed. Anyway, her mother was then overwhelmed by the task of raising six children. She had scant energy to spare fighting Wanda's battles at school.

Illiteracy had undoubtedly burdened Wanda's parents. Her father was a nonreader, as had been his mother before him. Not reading made it hard for the father to keep a good job, and he was under constant pressure as the head of a large household. One day he could take it no more. Leaving nothing to his wife and children, he just disappeared into the blue.

Wanda's mother could read but she had no previous experience working outside the home. The family went through excruciatingly hard times. There were days when they didn't have enough to eat. Wanda recalled occasions when she was so desperate that she furtively combed through trash cans searching for food. "I spent a lot of time then asking God why He was picking on me. It didn't seem fair. Thank goodness we weren't that poor for very long. I'm not sure I could have stood it emotionally."

"Tell me about high school, Wanda," I prompted. "Was that any better than grammar school?"

"High school," she began, "was hell. I hated it. I tried to be invisible when any teacher called on people to read. I probably came down with 'laryngitis' more than any other student in that school's history. No one wants a student who cannot raise her voice above a whisper to read to a group of high schoolers. I had a whole list of ways to hide my reading problem. On the other hand, it seemed that everybody on the planet was able to read except me."

As she said this, tears began to run down her lightly freckled cheeks. "I feel so unworthy!" she moaned. "I must be a bad person and that's why I can't read." Wanda's remark is not unusual for people with learning disabilities. I've had many students tell me they feel they are 'bad' because they can't read. For most people, in fact, discovering that they have a learning disability, rather than, say, a low IQ, is often a tremendous relief. Many had feared their failure was caused by something like a severe emotional disturbance, mental retardation, or damaged genes. But the most common fear is that they are somehow bad and undeserving. Some have even told me that God must have thought they weren't good enough to learn to read. What a truckload of guilt!

I looked Wanda square in the eye and said, "You've mis-diagnosed yourself. You have as much of God in you as anyone else does. It's up to you to learn to use what you have. You're as good as anyone, Wanda. You're not a bad person. You only have dyslexia. Lots of people have dyslexia. But many of them also learn to read. You can too."

Much later, while telling her story in front of one of my graduate classes, Wanda remarked that I had helped her the most when I said she had 'as much of God' in her as anyone else. Somehow, those words had made her begin to feel she wasn't 'bad' after all, and beyond that, perhaps God did indeed have a purpose for her in life.

After awhile Wanda introduced me to her husband Jim. I found him to be a kind, caring, stable man who was obviously good for Wanda. As a businessman, Jim was a terrific salesman and had a knack for getting along with almost anyone. His business grew steadily, so he and his partner enlarged their facilities. In time Jim and Wanda were able to purchase a lovely home in one of the best sections of town.

Wanda displayed a gift for interior decorating, and before long the house was beautifully appointed from top to bottom. The up-to-date kitchen was a dream for a woman who had come to enjoy cooking.

The marriage produced two adorable children: first Betty, who became quite attractive, and Artie, who soon displayed evidence of hyperactivity. He was constantly on the move, seldom tired, and never took naps. Artie might have worn out any parent who did not have the energy to keep up with him. Fortunately, Wanda had enough, although she was not hyperactive herself.

Nonetheless, soon after the family moved into their new home, Wanda started feeling progressively more inferior. "I saw," she remarked, "that my neighbors were doctors and lawyers. I was the only person on the block who hadn't been to college. I felt like I didn't belong. By and by I didn't smile much—unless I was making fun of myself.

"When my children started in school, I just knew they were ashamed of their mother. I especially felt my daughter's shame because she herself was a good student." Once again Wanda's eyes filled with tears.

"When is the right time to tell a person you can't read? I met new people who seemed to like me, but if I was going to see anything of them, I couldn't hide my reading problem. After all, if you go to lunch with someone, you can't just order the same thing the other person does all the time. It got to be easier just to say, 'No thanks, I'm busy.'

"Our house isn't on a bus route, so I'm really stranded. Before, when we lived in town, I rode the bus everywhere. If I needed to check a bus route on a sign, I simply asked a stranger waiting next to me. I'd say I'd just had my eyes examined and hadn't received my glasses yet. The selected stranger always seemed glad to help."

With Jim's support, Wanda took driving lessons. How she ever passed the written examination I will never understand, but she did it. Her driving instructor knew she couldn't read, so perhaps he convinced the examination officer to read the test to Wanda.

With laughter in her eyes Wanda told me about a trip to Cincinnati she made with the new Cadillac her ever-generous husband had given her.

"You should have seen us—my brother, my sister and me on the interstate. None of us can read a word. We fought most of the way about what the road signs said. My brother, for instance, would insist it was time to get off the interstate; my sister said, 'No, we should have gotten off one exit earlier;' and I just said I thought we were on the wrong road to begin with."

Wanda had a rare gift of bringing sunshine into others' lives. I eagerly anticipated our sessions together. I had never met anyone else quite like her. When she wasn't crying about how miserable she was because she couldn't read, she was more entertaining than anybody else I had ever known. Once she told me, "Probably the thing that has helped me most is that I can clown around. It just comes naturally. Somehow, I always come up with a funny remark and everyone laughs."

We continued to meet once a week. Each time I found myself admiring Wanda for her flawless smile, her wavy red hair and her perfect figure. I felt certain that she didn't realize just how attractive she was. Because of her parallel parking problems, I began going to Wanda's home for our sessions. After we finished our reading and spelling sessions, we usually sat and talked while she served me tea or a Coke and tempted me with something she had just baked. I was never hard to convince. One day when we met,

Wanda was unusually upset. She cried our whole time together. She was still, after all our work, convinced that she was retarded and worthless. What a letdown for me! I made an appointment for her to see a good clinical psychologist who had a special interest in dyslexics.

The psychologist, a Dr. Martin, was a Godsend for Wanda. His quiet, unassuming manner immediately put her at ease. She discovered she could confide in him. As I had found earlier, Dr. Martin learned that Wanda was very hard to test with any accuracy because of her extreme anxiety during testing. One just had to observe her behavior and make inferences from that.

Wanda met with Dr. Martin for an hour each week. As the weeks went by she became more relaxed and self-confident again. She told me at length that maybe, just maybe, there might be something worthwhile in her. And she grinned as she said it. My own efforts to persuade her of this prior to Dr. Martin's intervention had usually met with a hopeless stare or by Wanda's telling another of her put-down jokes against herself.

I tried to get Wanda to tell at least one other person about her dyslexia. It was important to stop her from covering up. For a time she resisted. Then, the day before Thanksgiving that year, she went to Jim's company to help distribute the turkeys that her husband always gave each of his employees. When she got there a foreman she knew came up to her with a big smile and said, "Hi Wanda! I've got something I want you to read."

She could tell it was something he'd found funny. As was her habit she could have pretended to read the item, laugh a little, and leave feeling awful for having kept up the lie. Today, however, she took a big step.

"Well, Lester… I wish I could read it. But I have dyslexia, so I have a lot of trouble reading. I'm being tutored and I'm learning, but I still have a ways to go." There! It was out. Having gone that far gave her courage to go on. "Will you read it to me?"

The foreman looked surprised. "You have dyslexia, too? My

brother has that, and my son also. Do me a favor, Wanda, and talk to my son someday soon, will you?"

Wanda promised to see the boy. She almost floated out of the building. The truth felt so much better than the lie.

That one experience changed Wanda. From then on she had no qualms about telling friends about her dyslexia—without shame.

Several months later, however, Wanda again arrived at our session in tears. (As she had by now developed more confidence in her parking skills, she had gotten back into the practice of seeing me at the university.) On this particular day she was concerned about her son Artie, who had brought home a failing report card. We agreed I should test him.

My tests showed that Artie had not been fortunate enough to beat the odds of his genes. He had a severe case of dyslexia, along with attention deficit hyperactivity disorder (ADHD). The school system re-tested him and confirmed my diagnosis.

A former student of mine was the LD teacher in that school. I felt that Artie was in good hands with her as his resource teacher. Time proved that indeed he was. Wanda, in any case, seemed relieved when Artie undertook special classes each day in the LD Resource Room. Wanda herself meanwhile was progressing in our work together. She learned to read and write a number of three-letter short vowel words such as *hot, sad, big,* and *red.* Then we directed our attention to "silent-*e*" words. One day Wanda breezed into my office and announced, "I went to the grocery store this morning, and I want you to know that I bought a box of rice without looking at the picture. I actually read the word 'rice.'" She was so excited. I found out later that she had exuberantly shared this news with everyone around her.

Gradually, it became apparent that Wanda needed more than the one hour per week of tutoring I could give her. I spoke with another former student who enjoyed working with adults. Could she work with Wanda twice a week? She could. I was relieved.

Wanda would benefit more, I thought, by having one teacher work with her over a longer period. So I decided we should end our own sessions together. It saddened me to stop my counseling and teaching with Wanda, as she had simply become part of my life. We vowed to stay in touch.

Wanda called me occasionally, usually when she was upset and needed a sympathetic ear. I will never forgot one call. "Barbara, I talked to Jim last night," she began. "I told him I didn't love him."

"My God, Wanda, why did you do that?"

"Because he's too good for me. He'll be better off without me."

"What did Jim say when you told him?"

"He stared at me for a few minutes, and then he cried like a baby. He begged me to say it wasn't so. Then he said he loved me enough for both of us and he didn't want me to leave. I told him I would stay."

Things at Wanda's home, however, were never quite the same after that. A distance opened up between her and her husband, and grew. A year later Wanda called me again.

"Jim says he wants a divorce," she announced, trembling with tears. "He has fallen in love with a doctor's wife and they want to get married. They've been seeing each other for months. Jim told me he would never have gone with somebody else before I said I didn't love him, and I believe him. Jim is very honest. But I just don't know what to do. I've never worked since we were married, and I don't read well enough to get a job that pays anything. What's going to become of me?"

I was stunned. What should I tell Wanda? Groping for words, I made a silent prayer that I would come up with the right advice.

"Jim told me to see a lawyer," Wanda continued. "He wants the divorce right away. Barbara, I haven't told you the worst yet. Jim has convinced the children that they will be better off living with him. Oh, Barbara, I can't lose my babies!"

"But Wanda, why would the children want to live with him

instead of you?"

"He's told them he can give them more than I ever could. He's been showering them with gifts lately. His girlfriend has a child, and he says they'll all have great times together. They plan to travel a lot."

I thought for a moment. "Wanda, probably the best thing I can do for you is to help you find a good lawyer. I know an attorney who has a relative with dyslexia. He should be quite understanding of your problem. We can go see him together."

She readily agreed to my recommendation of an attorney. But she said she would contact him by herself. A few days later she called to tell me that both Betty and Artie had signed depositions stating they wanted to live with their father. It would be very difficult for Wanda to fight someone with money and power. I was sure Jim's lawyer would tell the judge that Wanda was illiterate and could not help the children with their homework. That would not favor her appeal for custody.

A few weeks later Wanda asked me to accompany her to court for the divorce hearing. She arrived looking especially beautiful. No one looking at her would have suspected how frantic she was inside. As the hearing proceeded I read to her when compromises were written down on paper and rephrased for her the instructions her attorney was trying to give her. Wanda, however, was so distraught that she did not take in the details well at all. The judge awarded custody of both children to their father and allowed Wanda a small financial settlement. It didn't seem fair. When I left the courthouse I felt as if a steamroller had just run me over.

Wanda called me again when it was time for her to get a job. She wanted to know what to do when someone handed her a job application. I suggested she take it away with her and have a friend help her fill it out at home.

Several weeks later Wanda phoned to say she had a job sitting with an elderly lady. The lady had an apartment near a very lovely park a mile from where her children lived with their father.

Wanda, nonetheless, had great difficulty adjusting to her new life. Dealing with taxes, bills and all the 1,001 things in life all alone frightened her. She had always depended on Jim for such things. Her part had been to keep the house clean and attractive, do the cooking, and care for the children. Her husband had taken care of everything else. He had given her cash whenever she needed it to shop. How would she write checks? Keep track of her finances? She missed the security Jim had provided, and her fears kept her awake at night. In all her life she never felt so alone.

I didn't hear much of Wanda after that. And she discontinued her tutoring sessions with my former student. Occasionally, I wondered how she was doing. Once when I tried to call her, I found that her phone had been disconnected. I had never really known her other friends, so I had no idea where I might find her.

Several years later an aunt of mine fell and broke her hip. Upon her physician's advice she sought someone to stay with her and help her around the house. Immediately, I thought of Wanda. I was finally able to locate her after it occurred to me to contact her psychologist. Wanda's last elderly sitting job had just ended, as it turned out, and she was ready for a new assignment. Perfect! My Aunt Myra liked Wanda from the beginning. She enjoyed her vibrant personality, her attractive appearance, and her pleasant manner. Before long I noticed that Aunt Myra was helping Wanda with the grocery list and other written items. She also read the newspaper to Wanda. It was good for my aunt to feel she was helping someone. My aunt had worked hard all her life, as a businesswoman and a Red Cross Gray Lady. She needed to continue to feel she was contributing to something or someone. Wanda perked up.

Living with Aunt Myra soon had her looking happier and more confident. Still, there was room for growth.

Six months later Wanda phoned me and said it was time for her to move on. She wanted to be around people her own age. Besides, staying at Aunt Myra's had given her cabin fever. I could understand how she felt, but her departure from my aunt's saddened me nonetheless. I had enjoyed coming over to visit the two of them together. They had made a nice pair.

"Wanda, promise me you'll let me know where you are and how you're getting along," I said. "Don't just disappear off the face of the earth. I care about you, you know."

She smiled, showing off her beautiful teeth, and said, "Don't you worry about me, Barbara. I won't be too far away. I've got to find myself some romance before I'm too old to get around!" She winked knowingly.

Despite her promise, Wanda did not communicate with me for about five years. When I decided to interview her for *The Pretenders*, I located her by phone. She had settled in once again sitting with an elderly woman, about fifty miles away.

I asked whether she could come to my home and she readily agreed. What would Wanda look like now? I wondered, as I awaited her arrival. When she drove up in a classy, white sports car, I was thrilled to see that her beauty hadn't faded. Her gorgeous red hair fell around her face in flattering natural waves and, as usual, she was stylishly dressed.

I made coffee for her, tea for me, and we sat in my kitchen to catch up. Wanda told me that her daughter had been to college and was working as a laboratory technician in a southern state. Her son Artie, she said, had graduated from high school and was laying carpet. He seemed to like his job and engaging in daily physical work helped take the edge off his hyperactivity. Wanda did tell me that she had heard Artie drank too much. When she tried to talk to him about it, however, he laughed off her concern and told her he would stop, "when I settle down."

"Wanda," I ventured, "do you still feel your daughter is ashamed of you?"

"No," she replied. "I know I always told you that she was ashamed of me. But do you know what? She wasn't ashamed of me. I was ashamed of myself!" She smiled faintly. I became aware of an inner calm that was totally absent when I first met her.

"Getting me to tell Lester about my reading problem was just a beginning," she said. "And really, Barbara, today I'm not ashamed of having dyslexia. I tell my friends I don't read well. If they care about me, they understand. I've found that people will help you if they understand what your problem is and what they can do."

"I brought a videotape with me," Wanda added. "Want to see it?" She explained that she had participated in a pilot literacy program. At program's end, the students had made a videotape recording their reactions to what they'd been taught. I wasn't surprised when I saw how Wanda stood out as the most impressive person in the group. She spoke quite freely about her life as a dyslexic and how she had managed to survive. I felt as proud of her as if she were my own daughter.

This literacy program had been her first attempt to learn to read since her divorce. I asked if the program had helped.

"No," she said. "They just didn't teach me the way they should have. They tried to get me to memorize lists of words and then read them in a story. You know I can't do that. I kept telling my teacher I needed to have a phonics approach. I told her I had to write with my finger on the table top or in salt on a cookie sheet the way I did with you. But she didn't seem to understand. When I graduated from the program, my teacher gave me the book we had read together. She said she knew I would enjoy reading it to myself. Barbara, I can't read that book! I can't begin to read that book. Look at these words!"

She showed me a typical adult reader for beginners. The words in the book had been selected because they made a good story, not because they had a phonetic relationship. The program included no multi-sensory involvement to help Wanda with her reversal problem. And writing was not taught at all. I have found that writing down what one reads reinforces the learning experience, and the student retains information much better. Teaching reading, spelling, and handwriting simultaneously is a must when teaching most dyslexics.

Wanda's life seemed to be going along smoothly. She had a budget and stuck to it most of the time. One of her female friends stopped by several times a week to write checks and do any other writing that needed to be done — tasks that Jim had previously handled. Incidentally, Jim was married to his second wife for only seven years before they divorced. His two children became very unhappy with his new wife and her child. From what I heard, there was a great deal of friction. I have often wondered if Jim regretted leaving Wanda, and especially taking the children away from her. We can't retrace our steps, but I believe if Jim could redo the past, he would still be with Wanda today.

As Wanda was preparing to leave my house, she suddenly remarked, "Do you know, Barbara, life after Jim has been good for me. Working with elderly people has taught me patience and helped me become more understanding of others. I used to have far less patience than I seem to have today.

"I have a lovely house and a dog named Hugo. I named him that because he came to me during Hurricane Hugo. I call him my sausage dog, and I suppose I love him so much because he can read as well as I can — well, maybe not quite as well. He loves me and he doesn't lie to me. We're good friends!"

I've never known anybody quite like Wanda. I hate to think of what a miserable person I would be if I had gone through life not being able to read or if I had lost my children in a custody battle. But Wanda has risen above her own unhappiness by helping others. She seems to have found an inner peace.

I didn't want Wanda to leave. I was afraid maybe I'd never see her again. However, we hugged and promised to stay in touch. Then she closed the door of her white sports car and drove away, her red hair blowing in the breeze.

chapter 7

craig

DYSLEXIC STUDENTS SHOULD, I usually recommend, wait a year in their college studies before attempting an English course. They need to develop self-confidence before taking on the class that quite likely will be their most difficult academic challenge. Craig Brown, nonetheless, who was already enrolled in our H.E.L.P. Program at Marshall University, decided to tackle English composition as a freshman.

As it turned out, the understanding professor whose name was in the schedule had to back out of teaching that class because of another commitment. A part-time instructor was assigned in his place. This young woman was a stickler for correct spelling. In her opinion, Craig could spell better if only he concentrated more. No amount of my talking to her about dyslexia could convince her otherwise.

The English instructor insisted that Craig participate in timed writings in class, although he had a legal right to a time extension as guaranteed in The Rehabilitation Act, Section 504. Like many dyslexics, Craig is very creative, and the content of his timed writings was excellent. His spelling, however, was a disaster.

The day the class had a timed writing assignment as a midterm exam, Craig took his rough draft to the instructor for her comments, as she had requested of everyone; she made a few suggestions and turned it back to him. Craig then rewrote the paper and handed it in. The teacher read what he had written, made a very large red X across the middle of the page, and sighed loudly. She then tossed the paper onto her desk in disgust and said, "This is *totally* unacceptable."

Every student in the room looked up to see what was going on. Craig himself was floored by her behavior. He attended the class regularly. He took part in class discussions. He worked as hard as anyone else. Why was she treating him this way?

After the teacher threw the paper down on her desk, Craig picked up his books and left the room. He dropped the class that very afternoon.

When Craig came into my office, he was extremely agitated. His face flushed with anger as he talked rapidly in sentence fragments trying to tell me what had happened. I listened to his story, then looked at him, smiled gently and said, "Craig, you have been treated unfairly — even illegally." As he turned to leave, I told him, "You know, I'm convinced that God has some very special punishment in store for teachers like this one." He smiled weakly. Craig had already had many problems with English teachers in his scholastic career. He didn't need one more. But I persuaded him that this occurrence was only a minor setback. We would work on his dyslexia and his emotional reactions together; neither of us was ready to pitch in the towel.

I recalled my first impressions of Craig as a young scholarship athlete in soccer with special learning needs. He was a tall, muscular young man who was obviously very physically fit. When he came to see the soccer coach and me with his family, he walked up with a sparkling smile and a contagious friendliness, clasped my hand firmly and said, "I'm really glad to meet you, Dr. Guyer. I know if I'm going to do well in college, I'll have to be in a program like yours."

"Wow!" I said to myself. "What a personality."

I noticed that Craig asked very thoughtful questions of the coach, such as, "If I had an important test the next day and needed extra time to study, would you give it to me?" Not many incoming freshmen ask questions of that degree of sophistication.

The coach explained that there was a service available to Craig called The Student Athlete Program, which provided daily tutoring. Craig Brown's father said he and his wife would prefer to have Craig in a program geared to meet the needs of LD students exclusively. They felt Craig had been mainstreamed too much in high school; they were wary of a tutoring program simply aimed at athletes in general. I understood how they felt. We made arrangements for Craig to participate in H.E.L.P.

I turned to Craig and said: "I understand you have a brother."

"David, my younger son," Mrs. Brown interjected. "He was quite successful in junior high school. David's been deaf in one ear since birth, but his hearing's normal in the other ear."

"David and I always compete," said Craig. "That's been good for both of us. We always have to try harder because we're each trying to outdo the other."

After a cordial parting with Craig's family members, I had a chance to interview Craig in greater depth, and learned about his childhood trait of hyperactivity.

"My parents sent me to a nursery school that was very structured," he began. "My parents thought the structure would be good for my hyperactivity. I really tried to be good in nursery school. My teachers would tell me to *sit down!* and I would do it right away, but my feet would keep moving constantly, and my hands were always fidgeting with something. Also, I couldn't resist tickling my classmates, poking them in the ribs, or looking over their shoulders at their papers. Sitting still with nothing to do was too much for me. My mom said that I had a beautiful smile, though, and that helped a lot with my teachers. In fact, my nursery school teacher told my mom, 'This boy is going to be in politics. He has charisma!'"

Indeed, Craig did develop a knack for relating well to teachers. He tried to be sure his teachers liked him, hoping this would help win him a passing grade. And his likability did seem to help his grades—with everybody except for English teachers. In Craig's opinion, English teachers were in a different league. Thus he avoided taking English as much as possible. And he harbored special disdain for English teachers. Thinking this through a bit I came to realize that English teachers spent the entire class period focusing on an area where Craig had posted "No trespassing" signs ever since he was in grammar school. He had managed to survive by hiding his problems with reading and spelling. However, English teachers, Craig believed, had X-ray vision and could see right through him—revealing how inept he really was. To keep English teachers from seeing him easily, Craig developed the habit of sliding down in his seat as far as he could to escape their line of vision. Sometimes this worked.

In junior high school Craig was placed in a lower-track class. Unfortunately, testing in elementary school had failed to uncover his learning disability. Craig was extremely unhappy in the lower track. "What am I," he asked, "stupid or something?" Although he made much better grades in this track, he was despondent. All his friends were honor students, and he was embarrassed that he wasn't among their number.

In eleventh grade Craig's grades dropped considerably. The reason was that he had been failing to turn in his assignments. Nonetheless, when he arrived home from school, he would tell his parents that all his homework was done and then go outdoors to play. Teachers began calling his parents to inform them of Craig's failure to turn in his papers. The Browns were stunned. Why had their son lied to them?

Lying behavior is often seen among dyslexic or other learning disabled students in such situations. Perhaps Craig had been pushed beyond his endurance. Perhaps he knew he wasn't living up to his parents' expectations. While he realized that his parents would discover the truth eventually, he wanted to put off that discovery as long as possible. Craig wanted to avoid disappointing his parents. So lying was a way of stalling for time.

Craig

While Craig's English teachers seldom had any positive words to say about him, even his other teachers, while not as negative in their comments, usually perceived only the symptoms, not the causes, of Craig's problem. They came to regard him as the class clown, or the sleeper, or that evasive boy, or the easily-frustrated student. What virtually none of them suspected was that all these problems were caused by Craig's handicaps in reading and spelling. If those difficulties could have been detected and properly analyzed, much, if not all, of the "problem behavior" would likely have faded away. How sad. And yet, how often does such misdiagnosis occur in our nation's elementary and secondary school classrooms? Unhappily, regular classroom teachers rarely have adequate training to enable them to recognize the symptoms of learning disabilities—much less to know what to do to help.

Craig's parents then took him to a university for testing. There tests revealed that Craig's intelligence was in the superior range. They also showed that Craig had a learning disability. In language, his weakest area, he exhibited deficits in linguistic functioning, expressive language (oral communication capability), auditory retrieval (a way of recollecting certain kinds of information), following directions, syntax and grammar, and reading comprehension. He was not evaluated to determine whether he had attention deficit hyperactivity disorder.

The examiner felt that the reading comprehension problem existed because, as language becomes more complicated, it challenges people to develop more skilled understandings of grammatical nuances—and Craig had not developed these. Craig's reading, spelling, vocabulary, written language, and math were found to be two to three years below his grade level. His deficits in receptive language were especially significant and needed to be dealt with immediately because they affected Craig's classroom performance. Tutoring was recommended.

Craig recounted for me his reaction over being diagnosed as learning disabled:

"I was spaced out. I couldn't take it. I wanted to be like everyone else. To have trouble in school was one thing, but to be labeled as handicapped, that was something else. Other kids had trouble in school, but nobody seemed to label them the way I was labeled. My pediatrician, though, helped a lot. He explained what constitutes a learning disability; and he kept telling me I was very intelligent and bright enough to do whatever I wanted to do. But first, he said, I had to improve my skills. I had to learn to express myself better when I spoke."

The tracking at his high school, however, posed a problem. "At my school the mentally retarded kids and the kids with emotional problems were put in the same room as the kids with learning disabilities," Craig said. "I wouldn't go. No one could make me go in there. People made fun of anybody in those classes and nobody was going to make fun of me. I was going to make something out of my life, that's why I wouldn't go in there; I was going to show those teachers who thought I was stupid!

"In twelfth grade I was nominated for President of the Student Council. I worked my buns off trying to get elected, and I won. That was a mind-blower. But then the really hard part began: I had to learn to give speeches. Actually, this was a terrific break for me. My uncle, who is a lawyer, helped me get over my terrible fear of public speaking. He showed me how to outline what I wanted to say. After I'd written an outline, I simply memorized it. I'd then have to use just a few key words to keep me organized. My uncle also taught me how to look at the audience while I'm talking. He's been a lifesaver for me.

"I also had a lot of meetings with students who had complaints and with teachers and administrators. I learned to organize my thoughts before the meeting so I'd be prepared. Gradually, I learned to speak better. Now I think very carefully and form a sentence in my mind before I let it out of my mouth. Each year it's gotten a little easier for me to speak."

Craig experienced other successes as he moved toward the

conclusion of his high school years. For the senior yearbook he was elected Best Looking, Most Talkative, and Most Likely to Succeed. "That helped my self-esteem more than anything else," he told me, "but still I thought, 'I'm just not as good as other people.' I tried to ignore that voice in my head by staying busy, but it wouldn't go away."

He went on: "At graduation I gave my last and probably my best speech. The class seemed to like what I had to say. They gave me a standing ovation, so I felt that public speaking must be something I was good at. Some teachers even cried during my speech. Today I think public speaking is my greatest strength. That's a big change from the little kid in nursery school who couldn't speak in complete sentences."

Craig had learned to compensate for his academic deficits by becoming a good speaker. He had learned to speak up in class whenever there was an opportunity for discussion, so his teachers could see he knew the material. The only unfortunate fact was that Craig had never received the remediation he needed in high school to improve his reading and spelling.

When Craig arrived at Marshall he was somewhat wary. He covered up his wariness with a smile, however. He had registered for classes the previous spring, and his counselor had carefully selected professors who would be understanding of his learning disability. (Five years ago at Marshall a change was made in registration procedures to allow LD students to register one week ahead of other students, at the same time as varsity athletes. This very good idea is currently in force at many, though not by any means all, of our nation's universities and colleges.) The last-minute switch in English teaching assignments during Craig's first semester, however, caught us by surprise.

The semester following Craig's unhappy brush with the inflexible part-time English instructor we helped him enroll in an English class taught by a woman I had come to know and respect, Dr. Pendarvis. This professor was more interested in the content of a paper and did not let students' bizarre spelling ruin their grade. Dr. Pendarvis allowed Craig the time he needed to write and also permitted him to write his in-class assignments outside the classroom so he wouldn't be distracted. This was a tremendous help.

Craig seemed to be sailing along that semester when he suddenly developed strep throat. His tonsils became very enlarged, and a specialist told him they had to be removed. Craig went through sporadic illnesses from late January until he had his tonsils taken out during spring break. He had scant energy and lost a great deal of weight. When he returned to school from spring break, he looked pale and weak.

Dr. Pendarvis boosted Craig's confidence by complimenting him on the creativity of his papers. She wrote in the margin things such as "Insightful!" and "Clever!" She never penalized him excessively for spelling, though I'm sure she must have smiled as she noticed Craig's spelling of *friend* as *frenid*, *form* as *forme*, and *here* as *heir*. She gave Craig a final grade of C, and I heaved a sigh of relief. One English composition class down and one to go.

Craig tackled English 102 the following spring. Fortunately, he enrolled in a class taught by a very kind gentleman, a Dr. Ramsey, who had a special interest in writing skills and creativity. This professor led very lively discussions, which Craig joined quite willingly. Dr. Ramsey liked Craig's creative ideas for papers and was not put off by Craig's spelling problems. Dr. Ramsey's special interest was poetry and he included the reading and discussion of poems in his sessions. Craig, however, found poetry difficult. As he explained to me, "It's difficult enough for me to understand a normal paragraph, but it's almost impossible to understand poetry with all those hidden meanings that you've got to interpret."

Finding hidden meanings was not easy for Craig. But with Dr. Ramsey's help, he learned how to manage his assignments. He had learned, over time, how to speak well, and he would learn to cope with poetry, too.

What interested me most about Craig's relation to English

classes was his attitude toward the professors. I couldn't blame Craig for feeling hostile toward his first college English instructor with her inflexible approach to treating dyslexics just like other students in regard to their spelling. However, I knew that both Dr. Pendarvis and Dr. Ramsey had been exceptionally kind to Craig. They met him halfway and made every allowance possible for his learning disability.

Craig seemingly couldn't see this, though. Whenever I discussed his English assignments with him, he bristled and became defensive. This did not occur with his other classes. I began to ask him about his experiences with English teachers in junior and senior high school. As I had suspected, he had been embarrassed in English classes many times. He would be asked to read a paper aloud and the teacher would laugh at him or make sarcastic remarks. One teacher, he told me, even smirked, "How long did it take you to write that, Craig? Three minutes? Which member of our class wants to read a paper that had some effort put into it?"

Craig's scars in English, as anyone reading this might imagine, went deep.

When Craig came for tutoring, he often was so anxious about his classes that he needed time to unwind. His remediation tutor usually had trouble getting him to focus. Often Craig would complain, "I'm just too upset to work on that today. I just need to talk to you about my classes." The tutor would listen for a few minutes, then try to sneak in a little work on improving his skills.

When Craig took an exam, he perched on the edge of his seat looking as if he might just explode at any moment. He wiggled constantly. It was imperative for us to help him relax. Often a hand on his shoulder was all he needed. Sometimes the tutor needed to remind him that he already knew the information he was prepping: "Remember, Craig, you studied this on Wednesday and got all the answers right. I know you can do this. Just slow down and relax."

After Craig had completed a test that his tutor was proctoring, the tutor was usually exhausted because of Craig's excessive energy and short attention span. We usually allotted double time to Craig's tests—more than half of which the tutor spent trying to get Craig simply to relax.

When Craig was frustrated, he often blamed his problems with tests on his professors, rather than looking to himself for the cause. Frequently, he felt the professors were just picking on him or were outright unfair or incompetent. This was occasionally an accurate assessment. Most often it was not. Craig did, at other times, accept the responsibility for his troubles in class. He once confessed to a tutor, "My attendance hasn't been good. It's no one's fault but my own that I turned in a paper two weeks late. I can't blame the professor for refusing to accept it. She didn't accept other students' late papers, so why should she accept mine?"

After spending one semester on the soccer team, Craig decided he couldn't spend the many hours required in practice and still pass his courses. So he gave up the team. This was the first time since he was a small boy that he hadn't been required to train on a daily basis. He also stopped working out, devoting his time instead to studying. As one might expect, he became more and more fidgety, and his attention span decreased markedly. I noticed that his movements were jerkier than usual. When he sat down his feet were constantly in motion.

One afternoon I stopped Craig in the hall and said, "Hey, I've been thinking about you. Come on in my office for a few minutes. Let's talk." When we were seated I asked him, "Craig, how much exercise are you getting each day?"

"Not any," he responded.

"What effect do you think that's having on you?"

He paused to think, then said, "I find it harder to sit still. And it's almost impossible to concentrate for any length of time. It seems to get worse each day, too. When I try to study I think about my Fine Arts notes for a minute, then my mind is off and running on something else. Before I know it, I've gone down the hall to get some water. Then I'll go to the bathroom. Next I'll get a snack. If I need to call my girlfriend about a weekend date or something, I'll go do that. We may talk for forty-five minutes. One of the guys on my floor has been sick, so I might stop by his room to ask if I can get him anything. He's lonesome so I'll likely stay and chat. Then I might remember that I haven't done my laundry yet. So I'll gather up my clothes and haul them to the laundry. When I get back, say one of my fraternity brothers drops by. We'll talk awhile. Then I may remember that I haven't done any Fine Arts studying yet, so I make myself sit down and look at notes. But then my roommate turns on the TV. Well, I can't help watching TV for awhile. By now it's probably time for dinner, so I'll go down to the cafeteria. And I'll feel a little guilty that I haven't really studied for my Fine Arts exam."

Just listening to Craig tell about his afternoon made me exhausted. I noted that he often did not finish what he started. Such a random and often disconnected series of events is typical of people struggling with attention deficit hyperactivity disorder. They're always off and running with little direction or purpose. ADHD seems to be managing them instead of the other way around.

In the course of our conversation, I told Craig that I believed he had many of the characteristics of ADHD. He bristled noticeably. As I listed the symptoms I saw in him on a daily basis, I felt he was not listening to what I was saying. I continued, telling him that I knew many students whose grades improved significantly when ADHD was treated correctly by a physician who was experienced in this area. Craig wasn't interested. He told me that LD was all he could deal with, and that he would take care of the problem himself. I was not to worry. I didn't know what else I could do except wait for an opportune moment when he might be more receptive.

After I spoke with Craig he assured me that he would get back to working out on a regular basis. A week later I asked him how much time he was spending on workouts. He only smiled. "When

I have time," he sighed, "I exercise about an hour. But usually I'm just so busy, Doc, that I don't take the time."

I decided I'd better call Craig's parents. Normally I save calls to parents as a last resort. In Craig's case, I could see we were nearing that stage. Over the phone I explained to Craig's parents that I felt ADHD was his primary problem. The family lived in another state and getting to campus required an eight-hour drive. The following morning, though, Craig's mother came with her son to my office. When she and Craig engaged in deep conversation, it was easy to see that there was no hostility between them. Here was a good and healthy mother-son relationship. Craig needed to unload all his frustrations verbally and then analyze them with the woman who had nurtured him for so long and who cared deeply about his success. The two of them discussed Craig's hyperactivity and inability to concentrate long enough to study adequately or to research and write decent papers. Together they worked out a schedule that blocked out two hours a day of exercise for Craig. His mother and I then told Craig that this part of his schedule was to take precedence over everything else. If he didn't work off his hyperactivity, there wasn't much point in his trying to study. By the time his mother left, Craig had lost that defeated look I'd seen creep over him during the past month.

When Craig had exercised and wasn't upset or frustrated, he could usually attend to tutoring rather well. He asked thoughtful questions and was able to sit reasonably still for half of the one-hour period. He needed only infrequent changes of position or trips to the water cooler. When a tutor covered material that Craig found hard to understand, the tutor could explain it again and get it across. Craig would then restate the material in his own words, with no difficulty whatsoever. During these good sessions Craig was able to remember what was covered. He left the session feeling that time had been well spent.

Unfortunately, many sessions were not so ideal. Craig arrived in an anxious state. He couldn't sit still for more than five minutes.

He squirmed. His attention span was extremely short. Worse, he tried his best to distract the tutor and get the session off the subject. When Craig realized he had wasted a tutoring hour or when he received a test or a paper back with a low grade on it, he became terribly anxious. This anxiety only accentuated his problems with ADHD. When he took the next test, his anxiety would skyrocket. It wasn't long before Craig's tutors grew frustrated. One told me that tutoring Craig was like trying to nail Jell-O to the wall.

Thus the question of medication arose again. Exercise had definitely not worked for Craig. Modifying his behavior was to no avail. We had nowhere left to go but to ask a skilled physician for help. ADHD was interfering with his making good grades. For a student of his intelligence, a C average was not acceptable. He was certainly capable of doing better.

Then I had an idea. I was working with a medical student whose problems with ADHD were severe. It took me a year to convince him of the necessity of consulting a doctor regarding possible medication. But the results had been phenomenal. I called the medical student, who at the time was taking methylphenidate (Ritalin is one popular brand name.) He agreed to talk with Craig about his experiences with the medication. He suggested, in fact, that I have Craig call him, instead of vice-versa, so that Craig would be taking the initiative. He explained to Craig later how he felt he had benefited from the medication, and also discussed the side effects he was experiencing. This conversation convinced Craig that he should discuss his problems with attention and hyperactivity with a knowledgeable physician.

Craig's parents took him to a physician who specialized in treating patients with ADHD. The physician agreed that Craig would benefit from trying Ritalin, and he did respond ideally. He was able to concentrate for longer periods of time and was much less hyperactive. Craig said he felt relaxed for the first time he could remember. The best part was that his thoughts were no longer racing. We began to see a changed person with significantly improved grades.

It was a joy to watch as Craig began to use all of the strategies he had been taught through H.E.L.P., to wit:

1. Read textbooks and tests aloud to improve comprehension.
2. Visualize what is read.
3. Outline each chapter to structure what is read and make recall easier.
4. Use mnemonic devices when memorizing lists.
5. Adhere to a regular program of exercise.
6. Eat properly, even when overwhelmed with work.
7. Use breathing exercises to reduce anxiety, visualize success, and say aloud, "I know this material. I will do well."
8. Attend classes and tutoring faithfully (absences for illness only).
9. Participate actively in class discussions to show professors the material has been studied and learned and that the student is diligent.
10. Select understanding professors when possible and a balance of classes so there will not be an overwhelming amount of reading and writing during one semester.
11. Attend regular conferences with professors and never hesitate to ask questions.
12. Say, "*When* I graduate," not, "*If* I graduate."

It can be helpful for students to tell professors in their major fields how they plan to compensate for their learning problems in the world of work after graduation.

During his junior year Craig's sister, Eileen, a pretty and sensitive girl, had a life-threatening illness and Craig worried about her. He found it difficult to study for a mid-term exam in Marketing. When Craig's tutor, Ann, picked up the test, the professor gave her no specific instructions. The normal procedure, however, was that students wrote their exams in a class period, except for those enrolled in the H.E.L.P. program, who were allowed to take their exams at our center, proctored by a tutor.

The graduate assistant who administered the exam to Craig felt a great deal of sympathy for him. She could see how worried he was about his sister. She also realized he was so anxious about the exam he couldn't think very clearly. So she suggested:

"Since you can't stop worrying about your sister, Craig, let's do this test the quickest way so you can get it over with. Why don't we just make it an open-book exam. I'm sure the professor won't mind. And let's take it over at your apartment instead of at the H.E.L.P. center. That way you'll be less flustered."

So they went to Craig's apartment and Craig got out his textbook and began taking the exam in the kitchen. It wasn't long before one of Craig's roommates entered the kitchen and saw that Craig had his textbook open.

Craig's roommate, who had had to take the same exam in a class period and not open book, came to me Monday afternoon and told me what he had seen. I groaned. This could damage the reputation we at the H.E.L.P. Program were working so hard to build. I called the tutor but she wasn't home. My copy of her schedule indicated she had nothing until the next afternoon. All I could do was leave a message on her answering machine to contact me as soon as possible, at my home if necessary.

I called Craig and asked him to come to my office. When he arrived he looked very tired. He wasn't his usual hyperactive self.

"Did you take an exam in your apartment, Craig?" I began.

"Yes, ma'am."

"Don't you know that is absolutely against the rules we have about the administration of exams to handicapped students?"

"I didn't even think about it. I'm sorry."

"I spoke with your roommate. He thought something strange was going on when he saw you taking the exam in the kitchen. He didn't know exactly what you were up to, though. He was paying more attention to the football game on TV."

"There wasn't anything to see."

"Craig, are you trying to protect your tutor? If you are, don't bother. She's already in a great deal of trouble for giving you the exam in your apartment."

Craig looked at me with uncertainty.

"Did you use your book for the test?" I asked.

"My tutor said I could use the book. She knew that I already knew the answers. She said Dr. Cornwall wouldn't mind if I used the book."

"Did the professor tell you and the class it was an open-book exam? Did you hear the professor say that?"

"No, I don't remember that."

By now Craig was hyper again. "I've been so stressed out over my sister," he said. "I missed a lot of classes last week. Do you think I'll be thrown out of school?"

"I don't know what will happen, Craig. However, I do know you have to go to your professor immediately and tell him about how you took his test."

"Oh, no! Please don't make me do that. I'll throw up. I know I'll throw up."

I told Craig I would go with him. Then I called Dr. Cornwall, who said we could come right over. All the way across campus Craig said he knew he was going to throw up. He was a nervous wreck. Although I couldn't show it, I did feel sorry for him.

"Dr. Cornwall, I'm Barbara Guyer," I said when we reached the professor's office, "and I'm sure you know Craig."

"Certainly. Have a seat. So, what do you two have on your minds that's so urgent?"

I looked at Craig expectantly. "I believe Craig has something he wants to tell you."

Craig's face was crimson and his hands trembled. "Dr. Cornwall, I need to tell you something. I used my textbook on the midterm."

Dr. Cornwall smiled ever so slightly. "Only your textbook?

Why not your notes too? Why not the library?"

Craig added a look of confusion to his embarrassment and anxiety.

"Well, I don't know, sir. I just don't know."

Dr. Cornwall picked up some papers from his desk. "Let's see. You made a B-minus on the exam. That's better than the C you had on the first test."

Craig's face was even redder now. The flushing began at the collar of his shirt and spread up to his hairline.

"Dr. Cornwall, I'm so sorry I did this. I didn't mean to do anything wrong. If you have to throw me out of school, I'll understand. I've made a big mess of everything."

Dr. Cornwall smiled openly this time.

"I've had my share of students who cheated, Craig. They don't think it's very important. But I believe those students are developing behaviors which will follow them through life. Cheating on my little exams may not seem important, but it makes it easier to cheat on a business contract later. I'll tell you something, son, I have a lot more respect for you than I do for those students who have gotten away with cheating and think they've actually achieved something. You've had the courage to come to me and talk about it. You've been honest enough to own up to what you think you did. For that, I'm proud of you."

Craig looked at me. I looked at him. Our faces were probably mirrors. I felt the relief on mine which I saw on his.

"I like you, Craig. You're going to be a good business person some day. An honest one. I certainly appreciate your being honest with me. In fact, I really hope you take other classes with me in the future."

As we walked back across campus together I don't know who was more relieved. Craig spouted endless hyperbole about the greatness of Dr. Cornwall. After turning Craig down to a comfortable hum in my mind, I considered how impressed I was with how Dr. Cornwall dealt with Craig. In a non-threatening way he listened to possible violations; then he attempted to rectify errors, reveal their possible sources, and encourage Craig to keep up his good efforts. By the time we arrived back at the H.E.L.P. Center, I had decided Dr. Cornwall was a man of great understanding and experience. I was proud to claim him as a colleague.

The next day I talked with Craig's tutor. She said she thought Craig would be more relaxed in his apartment, especially since he was under such stress over his sister. She knew tests were normally to be given at the H.E.L.P. Center on campus and she had always done that. But she felt Craig's frazzled condition merited an exception. As for the open-book part, Ann said she distinctly remembered telling Craig, "I'm sure the professor won't mind."

"Ann," I responded, "I believe you were trying to be helpful to Craig; however, we cannot tolerate this failure to follow guidelines. Dr. Cornwall and I trusted you—we expected you to give the test as instructed. I'm sorry, but I can't renew your graduate assistantship next semester." It was difficult to do, but in our training sessions, I told our tutors that if they knowingly allowed a H.E.L.P. student to cheat, they would be terminated. I had no choice in this matter.

After Ann left my office, I leaned back in my chair and sighed. Although I regretted the entire incident, I felt lucky to have a colleague like Dr. Cornwall.

During his junior and senior years Craig was able to concentrate more on his major, Marketing, which meant he didn't have to take classes that were all different from each other. It was certainly beneficial to him when he didn't have to completely change his line of thinking when he went from one class to another.

Finally, Craig completed all of the course work required for a Bachelor's degree in Marketing. The night before graduation, H.E.L.P. held a reception for its graduates, honoring those who, refusing to give up, had reached this long-awaited goal. Each of the eight students said a few words after receiving a certificate signifying him or her as an alumnus of H.E.L.P. and, *ipso facto*, of

Marshall University. When it was Craig's turn, he left his parents, grandparents, and his brother and sister, and walked to the front of the room. His striking good looks and excellent posture gave him an aura of success. Or was it really that? Perhaps I had never before seen such sparkle in his eyes or pride in his step. Craig had the look of someone who had fulfilled a dream.

The room fell silent as Craig spoke:

"I wouldn't be here today if it weren't for some great people in my life and I want to thank them—my family, and especially my mother. She's always been there when I needed her. She never let me down, though I let her down a few times. I think my graduating from college actually began at my birth, because my mother has always fought for me, with me, and yes, against me when I was wrong. There was no way she was ever going to let me fail.

"Next I want to thank a very special professor who believed in me at a time when I wasn't making a very good impression. I have had many classes with this professor, and from each one I have gained not only academic knowledge, but the kind of understanding which will make me a better professional in my career. He taught me important lessons about something very simple: following directions. And one of the directions I learned from him, which he may not even know I learned, is how to find the real world. So often people will say, just wait until you get out of college and into the real world. Well, he taught me that the real world is wherever you find real people. Thank you, Dr. Cornwall, not only for giving the directions, but for being the directions as well.

"As for the wonderful tutors I've had, I wish I were an army general so I could give them each a few medals. They each deserve a medal for patience, and a sharpshooter medal for catching me when I tried to evade the help I needed. There would be several purple hearts too for valor in the combat of study halls.

"Finally, how can any student who goes through the H.E.L.P. Program not thank Dr. Guyer? I think we have to do that with our lives after we leave here, not just with words at a ceremony like this. Somehow she knew I could make it when we first met five years ago, and she always supported me, even in those times when I thought she was contributing to my torture. I had more problems in college than I want to remember. But, through Dr. Guyer, I gradually came to realize that I was becoming a stronger and more determined person than I'd be if I didn't have dyslexia. Dr. Guyer helped me see that having dyslexia has its good points, too. I have lots of energy, which used to get in my way. She has taught me how to direct that energy, and now I can accomplish even more than many other people my age.

"The H.E.L.P. Program has made it possible for me to graduate from college with dignity. Today I respect myself without qualification. I had successes in my life before college, before meeting Dr. Guyer and her staff at H.E.L.P., but I also had doubts about myself, about my real abilities. I am dyslexic, and I respect myself. I am dyslexic, and I don't even think about wanting to change that. I am dyslexic, and I'm ready to say here, for the first time, that I'm proud to be what I am. Dr. Guyer, you gave me that insight. I have learned much from many people, but it was Dr. Guyer who taught me, primarily by the way she always treated me, that I am the equal of anybody. She turned the question from what I could do to what I was willing to work to do. When I met her, the question shifted from my learning problems to me. In truth, after five years, I'm still not sure how she made that change in me.

"Tonight I will say, 'Thank you, Dr. Guyer.' But I promise to follow what I said earlier and let my life after leaving here be my real thank you note to you."

chapter 8

dave

ON A COLD, blustery, fall afternoon my office telephone rang and a distinguished voice began:

"Dr. Guyer?"

"Yes."

"I'm Ken Phillips, an attorney representing Dave Summers. Have you perhaps read about his case in the papers?"

"I've glanced at the articles," I said. I had noticed in the papers a case going on for about three months in federal court. Dave Summers was accused of selling dried up oil wells. Supposedly, the investors, aware that the wells had no value, were only looking for a tax write-off. The Internal Revenue Service had discovered that the sale of worthless property was becoming a common practice and was now cracking down on these frauds. Dave Summers, one of the first to be accused, had three partners. One of them had been given partial immunity if he would testify.

Then Mr. Phillips went on: "Three months into the trial I get the surprise of my life. I hand Dave something to read and ask him to comment on it. He tries to be evasive but I won't let him. To make a long story short, Dr. Guyer, I have spent six months with this man and today I'm convinced he can't read. I'd been suspicious about it before, but when I asked, he always assured me he could read. In fact, he's been a little too insistent. Anyway, what I'm asking you to do is test him. You see, he's accused of having written a fraudulent forty-page engineering report. From what I've seen of his abilities, however, I don't believe he could have done it."

We made an appointment for me to meet Dave Summers on Monday. Although I had tested many people of all ages, I had never before tested anyone on trial. I remembered reading in a financial newspaper that Summers had lost $17 million since the IRS started investigating him. How could a person who couldn't read amass that much money?

The next week I was walking down the hall to the copier room with a female graduate student when we saw an attractive, prematurely gray man enter the ladies' rest room. He didn't stay in there long! He exited with a red face and bolted into the men's room. I said, "That's probably the man I'm going to test this afternoon." When we returned to the Special Education Department, there was the gray-haired man. I bit my lip not to show I had recognized him earlier. And I dared not look at the graduate student—another bit of comic relief in one of my typically grueling days.

My motto is to laugh whenever you can possibly find anything to laugh at. When you consistently work with problems, you must laugh a lot in order to cope. I learned that the hard way, and so I teach students to learn to laugh at themselves. When they misread a word, it's helpful just to say, "Well, this is a great day for dyslexia. Mine is in full bloom!" Cut through the tension, laugh, and let learning continue. It's so much easier to deal with embarrassment and frustration with a touch of humor. When I get together with dyslexic students, we often laugh together. Sometimes we begin with, "Well, here is my story of the week. Who can top this one?" Sometimes I question the accuracy of the stories, as the students try to outdo one another. But it is so much more healthy to tell stories on oneself than to hang one's head and be ashamed of being dyslexic.

Dave Summers was far from joking about his reading problem and I wasn't about to suggest it... yet. In his face I saw a look of terror. Having to see me to be tested probably frightened him more than losing mammoth sums of money. It was difficult for him even to speak, at first. I invited him into my office, closed the door, and tried to look as non-threatening as I could. It seemed best to begin by not talking about him, so I asked about his family. Dave looked at me with alarm at first. Then he must have decided he could trust me, for he began talking. I soon learned he had a brother who was always outstanding, and parents who were both over-achievers.

He himself, he let me know, did not match up to his family. It wasn't long before he spoke openly of difficulties with learning the alphabet and problems with reading. His mother, an administrator in the public schools, had him tested many times, but no one seemed to know what was wrong, why he wasn't learning to read. Dave remembered being passed on to the next grade in spite of his lack of achievement, over and over again. While Dave was failing miserably, his brother was a perfect A student. Consequently, Dave's self-concept sank lower and lower.

In high school, Dave began to drink excessively in an effort to bolster his sagging self-esteem. Somehow he mucked through to graduation still not knowing how to read. Though Dave was convinced he was mentally retarded and absolutely worthless as a human being, his family assumed he would attend college. And so he enrolled.

While Dave had been shrewd in high school, in college he went far beyond mere shrewdness and proved to be a champion con artist. He taught himself dozens of ways to get out of reading, ruses which he could use at a moment's notice. Primarily, he became very skilled with the spoken word, because talking was the main way he learned to compensate for his reading deficit.

Dave told me how he avoided the Scholastic Aptitude Test, required of high school students before they enroll in college. "I promised the registrar I would take the test before the end of the semester," he recounted. "Later, when the registrar wanted the results of my SAT, I lied and told him I had sent in the registration form one day late and it wasn't accepted. But I could make up more of a story than that, so I explained how my grandmother had been critically ill, and I had had to spend a lot of time with her. The registrar didn't know my grandmother lived more than ten hours away from the school so, of course, I hadn't really seen her much. But the registrar was touched that I cared so much for my grandmother. As a result, he gave me one more semester to take the SAT." I could picture Dave smiling sheepishly as he left the registrar's office in triumph.

Dave told me about his study group in college. He loved the group and always wanted to be ready to participate since he learned virtually everything by listening to other people. He always seemed to know more than anyone else in the group, and if you didn't know Dave well, you would think he was an honor student. Since he couldn't read, he listened to every word spoken during class sessions and never skipped classes. Then he brought his phenomenal powers of memory to bear on the study group sessions and learned even more during discussions. Once Dave found out that most of his professors gave multiple choice questions, he memorized the key terms and tried to figure out the best answer without reading the question. Sometimes he was successful. More often he "lost" or "broke" his glasses just before a test. This made it necessary for someone to read the test to him. Once he broke his arm and kept the cast on longer than necessary so he could have oral tests. As Dave once told me, "If my arm had never healed, I would have had it made!"

Occasionally, Dave felt comfortable enough with a professor to discuss how he hated to read, but he never told anyone he couldn't read. He told several professors how he did so much better on oral tests than on written ones, and sometimes they would suggest giving him an oral test. Whenever this occurred, Dave made one of the highest scores in the class.

Dave said, "I began to realize that the only way I was different from other people was I learned by hearing information instead of reading it. But deep down inside there was a little voice that kept saying to me, 'Dave, you aren't worth a hill of beans. Anybody who is worth anything can read, and you can't even do that! You'll never amount to anything.' With thoughts like that in my head, you can see why I often headed for one of the local watering holes and tried to escape in alcohol. It didn't really help. But at the time I thought it did."

One of the experiences that stood out in Dave's mind occurred when he took German. He said, "I knew I had to pass German to be an Engineering major; and my teacher said I absolutely had to pass the next test in order to pass the class. When the test was returned, I saw *F* scrawled across the top. I got up and left the classroom without bothering to put on my jacket or even noticing the cold rain pouring down. I crossed the campus as quickly as possible so I could be alone in my room. After I closed my door, I burst into tears. It was just too much. I'd tried so hard, worked harder than anyone in the class, trying to memorize the spelling of the words. I remember picking up the German book and going to the bedroom window. I yanked up the window and began tearing that German textbook into shreds and throwing the small pieces out the window. As the papers fell, I saw my career as an engineer falling too.

"I'll tell you, Dr. Guyer, I couldn't have been much lower that night. I thought, 'Why is life so hard? Why does nothing work out for me? Why did God make me so stupid? I should just die and make the world a better place!' I even considered ending my life, but somehow I knew I couldn't give up. I just had to regroup and go on. After all, I could always talk my way into or out of almost anything."

Dave persuaded his parents to let him go to the beach that summer. There he spent the lazy days trying to forget college. He was very popular with the young ladies, and that was soothing to his ego. At least he could be successful here, and he already knew he could out-drink his fraternity brothers. He'd show these people just what he was made of! Stupid? He'd show them all.

At the end of the summer Dave knew he couldn't return to the college he attended last year. After all, he had never taken the SAT because he knew that would be a dead giveaway he couldn't read the questions. So he enrolled in a small college in a nearby state. The registrar agreed to let him enroll without the SAT, "as long as you take it before next semester." Dave used this approach four times—conning registrars into letting him delay taking the test—and he got away with it every time, only the campus was different.

While Dave was having so many problems in school, his brother was making a name for himself in college. He earned a Bachelor's degree in Economics (with honors), then a Master's degree, and eventually a Ph.D. His brother's success, although definitely well-deserved, contributed to Dave's continuing problems with self-concept.

Dave attempted to jump the hurdles of college, but he stumbled too often and had to give up that race. Still, his non-defeatist attitude and verbal intelligence made him successful outside academia. And his college experiences seemed to help, too.

When Dave mentioned he had a pilot's license, I asked him how he passed the licensing examination.

"I can't really explain it to you, Dr. Guyer," Dave said. "All I can tell you is I spent hours and hours memorizing the words I knew would be on the test. I never understood why the words said what they did. I just accepted that was what they said. When I took the examination, I couldn't really read the questions. But I could look at the words I memorized and pick the multiple choice answer that looked the most reasonable by the words I knew. I didn't make a good score, but I did pass."

I asked, "Didn't problems with reversals make it difficult for you to operate a plane?"

"Very difficult, if I had tried to read the directions and do what they said. But I couldn't do that. I had to memorize all the directions. My wife made a tape for me and I practiced the correct movements for hours. And you know, I bet I've never made a mistake while flying."

I said, "So the examiner never knew you couldn't read?"

"That's right. I never tell anyone I can't read. The only exception is my wife. I tell her everything. Even my secretary doesn't know I can't read."

I thought it sad he didn't share his secret with his secretary since she could be a tremendous help to him during a business day that otherwise might be very frustrating and even frightening. However, I could see that Dave was a person who had a great deal of pride—exceeded only by his lagging self-concept.

"Dave, how do you keep people from knowing you can't read? You must have developed a lot of tricks through the years."

"I have hundreds of techniques I use to avoid reading. They range from losing my glasses to having an eye infection to having allergy problems that affect my eyes. Sometimes I complain that my eyes are tired from so much reading and ask someone to read for me. That one works well because most people have had that experience—except for me. I doubt my eyes will ever be tired from reading too much."

Dave laughed then, and I saw his wonderful smile. His face lit up and his ice-blue eyes sparkled. He had that priceless quality of making you feel good in his presence. Because he relied on verbal communication, he knew all the tricks of communicating like a master. He looked at people intently when they spoke, and it was easy to see he was analyzing everything said in a way that made you feel important. Actually, Dave had the ability to listen to three or four conversations at the same time. When he left a cocktail party or reception, he could recite the conversations he had heard, even several conversations that had gone along simultaneously.

There was one thing, however, that didn't quite make sense to me. So I asked Dave, "I understand that you often flew to New York to close business deals. When you were on Wall Street, or elsewhere, and you needed to read a contract, what did you do?"

He smiled again. "That's easy. I simply asked a friend I respected to go with me. I paid all of his expenses and took him to the meeting with me. When someone handed me a contract to sign, I pretended to read it while making some humming sounds. After I'd examined the contract, I handed it to my friend and asked him to look it over. If he liked it, I signed it. Usually, though, I could take the contract home by telling the vice-president, or whoever, that I needed to think about it. I promised I would be in touch in a day or two. When that happened, my wife read the contract to me and I made a decision. It worked like a charm. No one was ever suspicious."

Talking with me about his reading problem had been an emotional experience for Dave, so I told him to come back the following day and we would do the actual testing then. After Dave left, I began to think of ways I could determine whether he would try to cheat on tests. After all, this time after testing I had to report to a jury, and I wanted to know the truth. I decided to give several similar tests. If his scores were not too different, I would be convinced that he was being honest.

Dave returned the next day. I don't believe I have ever tested anyone more anxious. He shook so hard I was afraid he couldn't hold the pencil. I had a problem with unsteady hands myself, so I understood, though I had never shaken like he did. Dave and I met in a room that was not only private but, fortunately, large enough that I didn't have to sit too close while testing him. Whenever possible, I moved to the other end of the long table. My sitting apart seemed to help his shaking.

The Wechsler Adult Intelligence Scale-Revised (WAIS-R) is the most respected intelligence test to give to adults who may have some type of learning disability. While testing, I was certain Dave was trying because he turned crimson when he didn't know something and looked as if he wished the floor would swallow him up at that instant. He was not to be that fortunate. I tried to reassure him as much as I could. When he knew he had made errors, I sometimes told him I didn't know the answer, either. Other times I told him if he were not a very intelligent person, he couldn't possibly have known that particular piece of information or solved that problem.

Because of the size of the room, I was able to get approximately twenty feet away from Dave while dictating the words of the spelling test. When he knew I couldn't see what he was writing, he became significantly more relaxed. I tried to look as if I were writing something unrelated to Dave, not paying much attention to what he was doing. I gave the mathematics test without picking up the spelling test. I could tell he was apprehensive about having me see what he had written, so I decided to let him keep all his answer sheets until the end of our session.

Dave scored at the top of the chart on some of the sub-tests of the WAIS-R; on others, he was near the bottom. I had never tested anyone who had such disparity in the sub-tests. The only part he had trouble with verbally, however, was the Digit Span sub-test, which requires repeating numbers, first forwards, then backwards. Also, when he tried to put puzzles together or copy designs, he fell apart. He rotated the designs (side up on top, for example) and reversed frequently. In spite of very low scores on some sub-tests, verbally this man was a genius. He received an IQ of 139 — right on the edge of genius.

As for Dave's spelling and reading tests, he scored in the second-grade range on all of them. His mathematics, on the other hand, was on a college level. If he had been trying to put one over on me he wouldn't have done so well on the mathematics test. I was convinced he was being honest with me. He really couldn't read beyond a second grade level.

I didn't meet Dave's wife until I went to the courthouse to testify as an expert witness. It was 8:00 AM when I arrived. Dave and his wife were in an outer room eating a breakfast of fast food and large Cokes. His wife, a professional person as personable as her husband, was an attractive woman in her late thirties with a warm smile.

Dave's attorney told me to testify first that morning. I had visual aids to show the jury the results of the tests. Carefully I explained that Dave was an unusually intelligent man who read and wrote on a second-grade level. I told the jury I had examined the report he was accused of writing and I testified that, in my professional opinion, he could not have written it. The members of the jury watched me intently as I spoke, but their expressions gave me no clue as to whether they believed me or understood what I was saying.

Two weeks later when I picked up the local newspaper, the headline read: *Dyslexic Convicted of Income Tax Fraud*. I couldn't believe it. After that, it was difficult for me to get Dave off my mind.

I decided to call Dave's attorney and ask him why he thought Dave had been convicted. He was quick to respond. "The case went to the jury on Christmas Eve, which can either set you free or send you up. In this case it didn't help. The first vote was eleven-to-one that Dave was innocent. The one vote for guilty came from a former law enforcement officer who said he would sit there for weeks but would never change his vote. The guilty votes gradually increased until it became unanimous. After the trial Dave and I were trying to decide whether or not to appeal, so we talked with a couple of the jurors. One of them looked at Dave and began to cry. She told him, 'I am so ashamed of myself. I voted you guilty because I wanted to be home with my family for the Christmas holidays.' It was hard to make the decision, but Dave decided the stress on his family wasn't worth it. He decided to go to prison and just get it over with."

The day before Dave was to leave for federal prison, I went to a restaurant and saw him there, by himself. He came over to the table I was sharing with my friend and mentor, Alice Koontz.

"Well, I leave tomorrow," he said. "Looks like I may serve three years. I've made up my mind about one thing though. I'm going to make good use of this time. I'm not going to be bitter. You can learn from anything you do; and I'm going to get everything I can from this one. I'm sure there's a reason I'm going to prison." (As it turned out, Dave would serve approximately eighteen months of his sentence, with time off for good behavior.)

"Dave, I'm so sorry I couldn't convince the jury," I said.

He told me not to worry, then went on: "I've been thinking about you, Dr. Guyer, and I believe you can teach me to read. A lot of people tried when I was growing up, but this time I think it will be different. You can do it. When I get out of prison, will you teach me to read?"

"Dave, I would be honored to be your teacher. Let me know when you're ready."

Several months later I received a telephone call from Dave's wife. "Dave asked me to call you. He needs some help. He wants to work on learning to read while in prison and wants you to send a letter to the warden stating what his problem is and what should be done to help him. Will you do that?"

The next day I wrote the warden, describing techniques I felt would work. I recommended tutorial help as part of Dave's program. The warden arranged for a remedial reading teacher from a nearby town to come to the prison once a week for an hour. Dave, however, did not like this tutor and explained to me:

"He keeps saying, 'I know very well you can read this, Dave. Now, show me what you can do. I don't believe that you can't read these sentences.' He treats me like he thinks I'm pretending I can't read. I've pretended that I could read all my life, but I'm not pretending any longer. I dread when he comes to see me."

Dave made little progress in reading while in prison, but when he was released, he called me right away. "I'm ready to begin to learn to read, Dr. Guyer," he said. "When can you see me?"

Dave arrived for our first session as I knew he would, feeling very anxious. I was a little uneasy myself because it's always difficult for an adult to teach another adult. Until that obstacle is overcome, the situation is far from relaxed.

Once Dave and I started working together, it did surprise me that he didn't know all of the alphabet, but not that he printed mostly capital letters very uneven in size. I decided to use the Orton-Gillingham multi-sensory phonetic approach especially developed for dyslexics. Letters are accompanied with sounds and clue words. I drew an apple at the beginning of several lines, wrote one cursive *a* and instructed Dave to write *as* across the page while saying the name of the letter, the clue word, and the sound of the letter. He could look at the apples if he forgot. After doing this with several letters, we were ready to blend three sounds into words. Dave had some difficulty with this, but he finally was able to say, "*f-a-t*, fat." Then I had him write the word he had just read. After several lessons of this, he began to catch on. I'll never forget the day Dave read a short paperback book that contained three-letter phonetic words. He put his head down on the table and wept. I patted him on the shoulder and said, "Dave, this is an emotional experience for me, too." The joy on his face when he lifted his head from the table was palpable—he all but levitated as he walked out of the room.

Since Dave was doing so well, I decided to give him some homework. He returned in the morning without the homework.

"Please, don't ever give me homework again, Dr. Guyer. Last night reminded me of the times I tried so hard to do homework when I was growing up. I couldn't and it made me feel stupid and worthless. Please don't ever ask me to do that again. I can't do it by myself."

"Okay, Dave, I won't do that anytime soon. But one of these days you will be ready to work on your own. You'll see."

Dave always came on time for our appointments, eager to learn. But one day he arrived looking very sad and more depressed than I had ever seen him.

"What's wrong?" I asked.

"I just learned my best friend has an incurable disease and won't live much longer. The one thing I'd like to do for him is something I am unable to accomplish… I want to write a letter and tell him what his friendship means to me — tell him I'm a better person because of him."

I thought for a moment. Dave had so much trouble thinking about what to write and then trying to spell it.

"Dave, how about this? You dictate the letter to me and I'll write it down. Then I'll dictate each word back to you and you write it. That way you won't have to think about what to write and how to write it at the same time. Let's try it, okay?"

"Might work. Okay."

So Dave dictated the letter and I wrote it down. When I said back each word in syllables, he sounded them out and wrote them down. It worked. Dave had his letter to his dying friend. We made many copies because we were so proud. Dave addressed the envelope. I wish I could have seen his friend's face when he received his first letter from Dave.

After one session Dave said he was in a hurry because he had a luncheon appointment. "Big business venture, Dave?"

"No, I'm having lunch with Father Joe from the parish down the street."

I must have looked rather surprised because then Dave said, "I've decided to improve my circle of friends. I got into trouble because I wasn't too choosy about who my friends were. I've decided to change that."

"Sounds like a good idea to me."

"It's interesting, Dr. Guyer, but since I'm learning to read I don't need to be the guy who can hold the most liquor anymore or be the biggest Don Juan in town. I suppose I'm learning to respect myself. Maybe I even like myself now. I've never felt that way before."

A few weeks later Dave arrived smiling.

"I went to Mass with my children on Sunday," he reported. "My youngest son usually helps me with the reading, but last Sunday I looked at the book, and all of a sudden, the words made sense to me. I read them without any help from my son! I stood in church and tears ran down my cheeks. I was never so thankful in my life."

Tears filled his eyes. I put my hand on his and said, "I'm so proud of you. You've worked hard and deserve to be proud of yourself. Knowing you has made my teaching all the more special. I'll never forget you."

Sometime later I invited Dave to come to one of my graduate classes and tell them about his life as a dyslexic. He came with his wife, Estelle, a rock of support and understanding.

"The woman must be a saint," I thought. Delightful though he is, Dave must be difficult to live with. I knew he was impulsive and headstrong and could get easily frustrated. Though, with his release from prison and his learning to read, his drinking problem abated and he developed into a faithful husband.

Dave spoke for over an hour, but my class barely blinked while he talked. Charisma hardly describes the appeal he had. He spoke freely of all his wheeling and dealing, his trips to New York, and his constant fear that someone would find out he couldn't read.

Near the end of his talk Dave said, "Oh, I almost forgot to tell you how disorganized I am. It's not unusual for me to have four or five things going on at one time — and I may not finish any of them. If I can finish something in a reasonably short period of time, I'm okay. But if it's very complex and needs repeated efforts over a long period of time, I'm in trouble. That's just the way I am. But I'm also very creative. It's not unusual for me to see a problem and then find a solution to it. For example, I invented several pieces of equipment used in the mining business and one in particular is used everywhere."

Dave continued, "I'm beginning to learn more about myself. I understand now that my behaviors aren't too unusual for someone who has dyslexia. I always thought I was really stupid, and I sincerely believed that was why I couldn't learn to read. Many people tested me, but before I met Dr. Guyer, no one ever used the term dyslexia or learning disability to describe my problem. And no one ever told me I was intelligent. In fact, I was told very little. I was left to make my own diagnosis, and I did: I arrived at the conclusion that maybe the world would be a better place without me, maybe I wasn't good enough to be able to read."

I broke in, "Dave, so many adults with learning disabilities have told me they felt they were bad people, not good enough to read. Reading is so important in our society that those who can't read develop social and emotional problems unless they receive help." I told the class how Dave himself was a good example of that. But he was working his way out of the hole he had been in, and the rest of his life would be much more enjoyable because he wouldn't be constantly trying to hide something.

When Dave ended his talk, my class gave him a standing ovation. I've never had a class do that for anyone else. He had them in the palm of his hand. And it was good for him, too, a catharsis after all those years of lying, hiding, and pretending.

Dave and I continued our weekly meetings for a few months, though I knew the need for our sessions was coming to an end. The last time I saw him, handsome in his English tweed coat, what made him look particularly appealing was the new sparkle in his eyes. When I mentioned I saw him reading the school newspaper while waiting for me, he said, "The words, too, not just the pictures."

I've seen Dave only a few times since then. Once in a while I get a report from a mutual friend that he has started a new business somewhere. Probably he will always be a wheeler dealer. Most important, Dave isn't ashamed of himself anymore. He doesn't have anything to hide, so he talks openly to friends about his lifelong problems with dyslexia and how he learned to read as an adult.

Sometimes, on days when the going gets rough, I remember Dave. The gray-haired man bolting from the ladies' room. The student throwing bits of a German text out the window. The reader with his face aglow with joy after reading a book of three-letter words. Or the writer sending his first letter to a dying friend. I remember, and the recollections bring a smile. Because of Dave Summers, I became a better person, too.

chapter 9

greta

THE LIVING ROOM was dark. It had been dusk when I returned home from work, and I had not yet turned on the lights. Blinking as tears burned my face, I sat there staring into the shadows.

How could I have been so blind? I kept asking myself, throbbing with anguish. For thirty-two years, how could I have missed the signs?

As I sat there deeply troubled, a scene flashed through my head, a scene from long ago—Mrs. Delaney, my daughter Greta's nursery school teacher, stopped me one day as I came to retrieve my little girl: "Barbara, did you know that Greta is rather immature for her age? She's obviously bright enough, but she's also very, very shy. And she cries so easily. Other children intimidate her without even trying. I'm afraid Greta may need more than one year in kindergarten."

Then Mrs. Delaney had patted my shoulder and smiled, "But you're a teacher. I'm sure you'll know what to do."

Now, over three decades later, one of my own employees at the Marshall University H.E.L.P. Program, Yvea Duncan, who had also become a friend, gave me test results on Greta that afternoon in my office. "Barbara," she said as gently as possible, "Greta has dyslexia. Not only that, she also tests positive for attention deficit disorder."

Slowly rocking in the darkness, I felt more like a failure as a parent than I had ever felt before in my entire life.

What kind of professional was I anyway? I had dedicated most of my career to the diagnosis and treatment of learning disabilities. Yet here was a colleague showing me that I had missed the evidence in my own flesh and blood—someone I had nursed and cared for, read to, and helped with homework all during her formative years!

My words to Mrs. Delaney's cautions about Greta echoed down the years to me:

"You're right about Greta's being shy. But you're wrong about her needing to be held back. Time will take care of her shyness. And I will work with her every single day."

I did know back then when we lived in Richmond, Virginia, that Greta had problems other than shyness. Being left-handed, for example, caused her some trouble with handwriting. She reversed some letters and made every s sideways on the line (∽). I kept trying to correct the way she held her pencil, but nothing I tried made much difference.

Greta had wanted so desperately to do well. She tried with everything in her. Sometimes when she made a mistake, big tears would fill up her beautiful brown eyes. At times, watching her like that nearly broke my heart.

The summer that ushered into kindergarten passed swiftly. And suddenly Greta was in the charge of a stern, elderly teacher named Mrs. Wilkinson. On the brink of retirement, Mrs. Wilkinson was a "no-nonsense" person not ready to brook many peculiarities in her young pupils. She scared Greta half to death.

In November Mrs. Wilkinson called me in for a conference. I was rather anxious, musing about Mrs. Delaney's cautions of the year before. Mrs. W got right to the point: "I want you to look at this drawing Greta made of a person." I looked at a stick figure with hands emerging from the shoulders. "Now," she continued, "these are pictures other children drew." I realized that the other children's pictures showed more maturity than my daughter's drawing, but then Greta was left-handed. It took longer to catch on to proportion and details when you were left-handed. Everyone knew that, didn't they? Everyone, that is, except Mrs. Wilkinson.

"Mrs. Guyer," said the steely Mrs. Wilkinson, "in my opinion Greta will not be ready to go on to first grade next fall. I believe she will be much better off repeating kindergarten. Her handwriting is poor and she has so much trouble paying attention. But there's really no problem that another year of maturity won't solve."

I stared at her hard. Was this my child she was talking about? How could this woman be saying these things to me? Repeat kindergarten! That would absolutely break Greta's heart. No! No! No! All she needs is a little time. Oh God, don't let them hurt her!

Back in my car after the conference, it struck me that I myself had not had a picnic of it in kindergarten. Miss Weitzel, my very devoted teacher, saw to it that I went to speech therapy regularly. I also remembered how learning to read had come hard for me. But I finally caught on and then excelled in school. Greta would do the same. We'd show Mrs. Wilkinson.

When I told my husband Ken that evening about Mrs. Wilkinson's comments, he was furious. How dare anyone criticize his daughter's drawings as early as November! How could Mrs. Wilkinson talk about a child's needing to repeat a grade even before Christmas vacation had arrived? I could only agree.

Though her final kindergarten report card indicated many weaknesses, Greta was indeed promoted into first grade. "Never you mind," I thought, "we'll work together over summer. When fall arrives, Greta will be ready."

If Mrs. Wilkinson had frightened Greta, the teacher our little girl encountered in first grade totally petrified her. Stern and rigidly strict, and also in her final year before retirement, Mrs. Adams, a large and intimidating personage, tolerated little movement in her classroom. Children spent hours cooped up in their desks with papers, pencils, and books.

Greta developed stomach aches. Fairly often we received calls from school telling us that Greta was ill and needed to be picked up.

While Greta attended Mrs. Adams' first grade class, our younger daughter, Jennifer, went to a Montessori school, a school in which children helped one another and competition was non-existent until the later school years. Jennifer blossomed in the Montessori environment—so much so she eagerly bounced out of the car each morning, happy to be at school. Greta, on the other hand, had a pathetic, pleading look in her eyes as she left the car to join children on the playground of the private girls' school where Mrs. Adams taught. But then, I told myself, Greta was quiet and shy, while Jennifer was more extroverted and ready to take life by the horns.

One day the principal of Greta's school approached me. "I'm afraid," she said, "that your Greta's an easy mark for the other students. They pick on her and make her cry very easily. Greta needs to learn how to keep them from getting the best of her."

When Greta's stomach aches persisted, we took her to our pediatrician, Dr. Bundy. A wise, folksy gentleman, he quickly surmised that Greta's abdominal pains were being caused by frustration and unhappiness at school. He gave Greta a sampling of antacid tablets and told her: "I want you to take one of these whenever you feel a stomach ache coming on. I'll give you a note for your teacher so she'll let you keep these pills with you."

Greta smiled as Dr. Bundy handed her the pills. She carefully put them in her little purse. She took the tablets for two or three weeks. We heard nothing more about stomach aches that year.

The day before Christmas vacation was to end, Greta suddenly announced that she was supposed to have read a book of 237 pages before she returned to school. She'd had the entire vacation period to dig into it, but she had "forgotten" to tell me—and no, she hadn't even begun. The book had quite a few pictures, but not nearly enough. Greta became frantic. Mrs. Adams would be very upset with her if she hadn't read the book.

"We can do it!" I told Greta, ridiculously confident of my ability to get my first-grader through a whole book in one evening. Soon after she began reading to me from the book, I decided we'd better fudge a bit. Greta read a page aloud, then I read one. The more she read, the more tired she became. And I could see she was getting very little from what we were reading. I pretended I was excited about the stories, which I really found quite boring. Soon I was reading two pages to Greta's one. When my daughter wasn't looking, I turned several pages at a time. When her eight-thirty bedtime arrived, I tried to persuade her to stop. She wouldn't hear of it. Greta was going to finish that book or not return to school the next day, and that was that. We read together off and on until eleven o'clock. When we finished the last page, we were both exhausted.

Greta went to school the next day, clutching the book to her chest. As irony would have it, Mrs. Adams was out ill that day. When she returned the following day, she must have forgotten about the reading assignment; she never asked for it, that day or any day thereafter.

Greta's first grade year was full of homework which she, her father, and I struggled through together. It was a long year. Greta seemed to spend a lot of it sick, despite Dr. Bundy's efforts. Her sister Jennifer, meanwhile, was moving joyously through her Montessori activities. We wanted Greta to try Montessori too, but we discovered that older students were not accepted until the sixth grade.

Near the end of that year Mrs. Adams asked me in for a conference. I went dreading she'd tell me Greta had to repeat first grade. Instead, Mrs. Adams said Greta had made a little progress, so perhaps she could try second grade in the fall. If she didn't fit in, they could always send her back to first. As I stood at her door poised to take my leave, Mrs. Adams stopped me: "I believe you should recognize, Mrs. Guyer, that your daughter may need to repeat a grade some year. She may just barely survive year after year, but the time will probably come when it will be to her advantage to repeat."

I fervently hoped that time would never come. Already Greta was tall for her age and shy. It saddened me that in no conference had a teacher ever mentioned Greta's above-average intelligence; they all focused on her weaknesses.

In second grade Greta struck gold: her teacher was young, vibrant Barbara Jameson, a woman I already counted among my friends. A jewel with a lovely sense of humor, Barbara allowed much more freedom, talking, and other activity in her classroom. She even let the children chew gum, as long as they didn't blow bubbles or pop the gum.

Greta's health took a swift turn for the better. I was so grateful to Barbara for my daughter's happiness that I wanted to hug her every time I saw her. Even Greta's writing improved; now she reversed letters only infrequently. More importantly still, Greta actually began to participate in class discussions. She found new joy in playing with her classmates. Invited to another child's birthday party, she went in a gleeful mood and joined in the fun. Our shy daughter seemed to be finding her place. Perhaps we were out of the woods.

Unhappily, events proved otherwise. Teachers for the third, fourth, and fifth grades were closer in temperament and style to Greta's kindergarten and first-grade teachers. Greta worked hard at homework, sometimes from the moment she arrived home until she slipped into bed. She seldom took time out for play, except for thirty minutes a day of physical activity that I insisted she do when she got home, since I knew she sat at a school desk most of the day.

When sixth grade arrived and the Montessori school became an alternative, Ken and I decided that Greta might be happier there with her sister, in an atmosphere of liberating flexibility, movement, and active learning. From day one at Montessori, Greta was ecstatic.

Two young men—a teacher and his assistant—led her classes.

They were very upbeat. Greta enjoyed the innumerable activities, and her skills improved markedly.

With several other students, Greta helped write a play about Thomas Jefferson, shared (with mothers) in the making of costumes, helped create scenery, planned a reception and learned a great deal about colonial history. The dress rehearsal was a typical comedy of errors, but the actual performance was a perfect delight. The children were so proud they glowed. I don't believe I have ever been so happy to be at a school, either before or after that evening.

Greta had written a significant chunk of that play. She was really blossoming now that she was so much happier than she'd been in a traditional classroom. Ken and I even noticed some leadership qualities in her that had been under wraps before.

Artistic of bent, Greta loved music and happily embarked upon the piano. Jennifer also took lessons but lacked Greta's enthusiasm. Whenever the girls had their lessons with Mrs. Childs across the street, our black cat, Herman, followed them. Herman sat on Mrs. Childs' windowsill while piano music floated out to him. He never sat there for anyone else's lessons, and always came right home with the girls. We often laughed about Herman the music-loving cat. At home, whenever anyone forgot to put the cover over the piano keys, Herman jumped onto the keys and walked up and down, seemingly enjoying the "music" he made with his paws. We joked about sending him over to Mrs. Childs for lessons.

Near the end of Greta's sixth-grade year, Ken told us about an opportunity he'd been exploring to move to a smaller city. For eleven years he had tried to make his peace with the Richmond metropolitan area (of about four hundred thousand people). He spent his early life, however, in a smaller town in the Texas panhandle, and it left him hankering for less traffic, pollution, and crime. Learning that a new medical school was to open soon at Marshall University in Huntington, West Virginia, Ken applied and found that they definitely wanted his expertise. I was skeptical. I felt it was important not to move Greta just when she was beginning to enjoy school. Upon reflection, however, I came to understand how unhappy Ken had been.

I knew no one with a husband more loving and dedicated than Ken was to me—nor a better father. I certainly could never have completed a doctorate in education at the University of Virginia, nor worked as a teacher and later as a principal in the Richmond public schools without Ken's unflagging support. The girls and I owed it to Ken to try living in a smaller city.

That August we moved to Huntington—fearful, excited, and more than a little apprehensive about the girls' schooling.

We had barely gotten settled in our new home when school problems cropped up for both Jennifer and Greta.

Jennifer's problems stemmed from being in a traditional classroom for the first time. She had been accustomed to planning her own day, with a modicum of direction. She had always competed against herself rather than with her peers. She helped her peers whenever they needed help, and they helped her in return. Now, on several occasions, she had been reprimanded for helping students who couldn't read as well as she. One evening I had Jennifer visit one of my graduate classes on learning disabilities, so she could talk about her years in a Montessori school. When one of my students asked her the main difference between a Montessori school and a regular classroom, Jennifer said, "In the Montessori school you help other kids. In a regular school they call that 'cheating.'" My students fell into a stunned silence. Unfortunately, what Jennifer said was true.

Since there was no Montessori school in Huntington, I took Greta to the neighborhood public junior high school to register. As we entered the building, the entire football team happened to be milling around in the hall in their practice uniforms. They uncorked a volley of whistles and catcalls over Greta. My daughter wanted to shrink into the floor. This was her first exposure to a large school.

I warned Greta's homeroom teacher that Greta's shyness might pose some problems. She just smiled at me and said, "Everything's going to be okay." Yet the very first day of school Greta had to be escorted to a counselor's office because she couldn't stop crying. The counselor, Mrs. Fillinger, turned out to be a blessing.

One day Greta accidentally pushed her locker door back too far and the door hit a boy standing on the other side. He blurted out angrily, "Hey, girl, what's the matter with you?! You retarded or something?" Devastated, Greta fled to Mrs. Fillinger's office. Mrs. Fillinger called me right away and asked permission to test Greta's IQ. "I want to prove to her that she's anything but retarded," the wise counselor said. Soon Greta was participating in the Gifted and Talented (GT) program.

Though I was pleased that Greta's finer qualities were being recognized, I noticed that Greta herself had not changed much. She enjoyed her GT classes, but seemed intimidated by her gifted peers. And school in general was an emotional strain. Ominously, her stomach aches returned. Sometimes she'd get so upset she would throw up. Many mornings Greta lay on the sofa in the family room waiting for her ride to school while I sat holding a cloth on her forehead trying to calm her down.

Eventually, with an abundance of help from Mrs. Fillinger and from Greta's school friend, Amber, Greta managed to relax. Her grades were usually unstable—unpredictably high or low, though in eighth grade she rocketed to a 3.9 grade-point average.

By high school the nausea and crying had ended, but Greta's shyness remained. So did the emotional stress. She continued in GT in high school, yet her grades remained unpredictable. She would often get a C in a class I thought would be easy for her. Frequently, she brought home tests full of careless mistakes. Despite knowing a range of material well, she was a master at putting down the wrong answers on multiple-choice tests. Ken diagnosed the problem as follows: Greta had so little faith in herself, he reasoned, that she would assume she didn't know the correct answers; so then she would change her right answers to wrong ones.

She kept up her music and her art, however, and her overall academic performance was above average. She grew from a shy, little girl into a shy young lady. I was glad to see her do some dating and even attend a prom.

When the time came to apply to colleges, Greta set her heart on just one women's college in Massachusetts. Her interviews went well. Both the head of admissions and the school's director of studies liked Greta; the director was especially pleased that Greta had attended the private school in Richmond. When the letter arrived from Massachusetts, Greta was so excited she could hardly open the envelope. She was also afraid. Many students, she knew, had better strictly academic records. Greta's outstanding qualities manifested more around the edges, in nuances.

The head of admissions informed her they could not accept her for the fall semester, which was full; they could, however, get her in for the spring. Greta would be spending four years in a good school—and her first choice. I had to admit I was proud—a mother's legitimate vindication of a talented daughter whose talents had gone too little appreciated. Greta was excited, too, but also demure, as was her fashion.

For the fall semester Greta decided to enroll for a class at Marshall and transfer her credits in the spring. I was not surprised to learn that her ACT scores qualified her to take Honors English. I offered to help her with her papers, but she made it clear she wanted to do this on her own. She often turned in papers that were difficult to read and sprinkled with small errors. Her final grade was seventy-five, which gave her six credits of C. I wondered why she hadn't done better.

In the spring Greta went away to college in Massachusetts and majored in biochemistry. She showed a sincere interest in her science courses, but rarely got more than a C. Greta often put things off until the last minute. As a student she seemed careless, lethargic, and procrastinating. Many professors commented about what a lovely, talented person Greta was, though many added they thought she was capable of better work. On the other hand, her chosen college was very competitive. When she ended her college program with a C average, I reasoned that my daughter's low-key, noncompetitive approach was primarily responsible for her low average. Somehow, I just never thought of ADD.

Just as her sister Jennifer became set on studying law, Greta decided that she wanted to go to medical school. Since no medical school would accept her with such low grades, Greta determined to pursue a Master's degree in physiology to improve her grades and prove herself a worthy candidate. She chose to live at home and attend the Marshall University School of Medicine as a graduate student.

Greta started working harder at academics. With almost superhuman effort she notched an A in biochemistry, far above what she'd done in that subject in college. The A seemed to give her hope and spurred her to greater efforts. She spent many hours studying at her bedroom desk or at the dining-room table, her cat curled up in her lap. I had never seen Greta study for such long periods at a stretch. I was not certain, of course, exactly how much studying got done, but Greta did sit there with her books and take notes while reading a chapter. Think what I might, in two years she completed her Master's Degree with a 3.5 grade-point average.

Greta had to take the Medical College Admissions Test (MCAT) twice. The first time, during her senior year of college, her low scores made it pointless to apply to any medical school. After studying intensively on her own, however, and also taking a course aimed at improving MCAT scores, Greta raised her level significantly—and was accepted to medical school at Marshall. Triumph!

Greta was never in serious trouble in any of her classes during her first two years of medical school. But she wasn't setting the world on fire either. Typically, she would make an occasional B, with the majority of grades falling in the C range. I looked over some of her multiple-choice tests and found it hard to understand why she blacked in some of the responses she did.

She proved maddeningly inconsistent. When she took biochemistry again in medical school, for instance, she received a B, even though she earned an A in the same course as a graduate student. Furthermore, she had retaken the course from the same professors — one being her father! Ken and the other professors treated her fairly and objectively when they gave her the first A; they also evaluated her grades carefully when giving her a B the second time. When Ken attempted to review a test with Greta to show her why she missed certain questions, she reacted negatively. He found it impossible to discuss any scientific topic with her for very long, because she would become evasive. Frequently, her response to being asked any medical question was simply, "I don't know."

Ken and I felt the problem lay in shyness and low self-esteem. We arranged for Greta to start seeing Dr. Joe Mock, a very skilled clinical psychologist in town.

Seeing Dr. Mock helped. Greta soon became more outgoing — and less evasive. She developed pride in her work as a medical student, and her grades went up.

At the end of her second year of medical school, however, Greta had to take the Medical Licensure Examination(MLE). She failed it. After crying for awhile, she dried her eyes, put her shoulders back, and got a determined look on her face. She would pass that test the next time through. Dr. Brown, Dean of Students, later told me, "Barbara, I talked to several students who failed the MLE today. I want you to know that Greta was the only one who had already mapped out a plan of attack. It was a breath of spring having her in my office. I'm encouraging her to take the test again in September, earlier than what I told the other students. She'll make it."

Greta threw herself into studying with a furor I had never seen before. She enrolled in a special course to help her prepare and studied every day that summer for hours. In September she took the MLE again—and passed.

The good times were back. During her third and fourth years of medical school Greta made all A's and B's. And she excelled at interacting with patients.

After graduating from medical school in 1990, Greta was awarded a residency in Internal Medicine at Bowman Gray Medical School in Winston-Salem, North Carolina, her first choice. She did very well there and received high commendations. She also met and fell in love with the man who would become her husband. Upon deciding to marry, Greta moved to Charleston, West Virginia, to finish the remaining two years of her residency.

As the day approached for Greta to take the Internal Medicine Specialty Boards, a two-day ordeal, she grew anxious and found it difficult to eat. She cried easily and became jumpy. When she lost weight, I urged her to go back to see Dr. Mock. She did and came away from their sessions with renewed energy and confidence— and more relaxed. To prepare for the Boards she also took a special course and studied tirelessly. Yet when she finally took the test, her scores were discouragingly low.

Greta was given a year to study to retake the Boards. Always a person of great determination, she launched into a carefully organized program, including two week-long courses geared to the exam. Hardly a day passed that didn't find her immersed in the books. She also scheduled time with Dr. Mock, leaving no stone unturned in her effort to conquer that exam. Dr. Mock felt that she was in good shape emotionally as her re-test approached, and wished her well. But she failed her Boards the second time, too.

Greta's scores had improved significantly, but not enough for a passing mark. Broken-hearted and humiliated, she dreaded telling her department chairman the news.

The physicians with whom she worked were puzzled. They

could see that Greta had exceptional rapport with patients, and she certainly seemed to know the technical material. Her diagnostic skills seldom went off base. Why, then, was she failing this crucial test?

Greta regained her composure and soon mapped out a line of attack. This time she turned to Yvea Duncan, a friend and very insightful Learning Disabilities Specialist who coordinated our Medical H.E.L.P. Program at Marshall. Greta asked Yvea to help her improve her strategies for taking tests. Yvea gladly volunteered to work with my daughter on weekends.

After a few sessions with Greta, Yvea came to my office at H.E.L.P. and said, "Barbara, we need to do some in-depth testing of Greta. I'm seeing signs of dyslexia and attention deficit disorder. If that's confirmed, this may explain why she's continuing to fail her Boards."

My jaw dropped. "Are you serious, Yvea, symptoms of dyslexia and ADD? I find that hard to believe."

Greta was tested over a two-day period. Her IQ ranked in the very superior range with a thirty point differential between Verbal and Performance IQ levels—the equivalent of two standard deviations. Something like this would occur with less than two percent of the population. Her reading comprehension was poor, her reading speed slow, her spelling at times bizarre. And evidence of ADD was definitely manifest. A ninety-minute session with a psychiatric specialist on ADD confirmed the diagnosis. He prescribed Ritalin.

Badly shaken, I sat at my desk fighting back tears. What flashed through my mind were images of hundreds of conferences with parents. I remembered my advising them, in all cases, to get help as early as possible. What in my own daughter I had labeled as "shyness" was actually "distracted-ness." Her mind was somewhere else because of not being able to focus. Under that quiet surface was a mind racing, always racing, with nowhere to go.

While I found myself plunged into personal and professional doubts and second guessing, Greta seemed rather relieved when she learned of the diagnosis. For so long she had wondered why she seldom did consistently well in academics when, deep inside, she knew that she had mastered the subject as well as her classmates. In just a few days Greta reported great improvement in her ability to concentrate. One morning after church she said: "You know, Mom, this is the first time I've been able to follow a sermon all the way through. I used to be able to manage about half. I'm sure glad that whatever it was is gone. Now I can focus for a long period of time. It's such a great feeling!"

As we drove home from church, I remembered Jeff, a student whom I encouraged to see a physician about ADD. After two years of traumatic experiences in college, he finally decided to follow my advice. The physician prescribed Ritalin. A week or so later I arrived early for work, well before eight in the morning, and was surprised to find someone there ahead of me. Jeff was quietly reading in one of the study rooms, so I poked my head in the door. "Jeff, why in the world are you here studying so early?" I said. "That's not like the Jeff I know. Who are you, anyway?" I winked at him.

Jeff smiled and said, "I just couldn't sleep any longer, Dr. G. I spent the first eighteen years of my life not being able to study. Now, with this medication, I can study for hours at a time. I'm soaking up this history homework like a sponge." He paused and then said, "I have a lot of catching up to do. I guess I'm just anxious to get at it."

Not wanting to interrupt him further, I smiled and went on my way. What a joy it must be to be able to focus for the first time in your life. Today, Jeff is a successful law student, and it is doubtful he would be there if not for the medical treatment of ADD.

I glanced at Greta. Her expressive brown eyes gleamed as she contemplated a future with the ability to concentrate the way other people do. "Just think what my grades could have been," she exuded, "if I had always been able to focus like this!"

Perhaps coming home from church is as good a time as any to confront guilt. We are not Catholic, but going to church implies a kind of confession that we aren't perfect; consequently, we all make mistakes of one sort or another. Ironically, the sermon that day had been about how the past and the present cannot be separated, but both are part of a larger whole that is our life.

I looked out the car window and let the details of the world slide by. I noticed colors more than actual things, especially the green of trees. Then the blue sky absorbed me. I averted my face from the window when the sun surprised me by bursting through a small cloud and beaming straight into my eye. Then I heard gentle singing. Ken and Greta were softly humming a hymn from the service. I wondered why I didn't join them.

I realized then that neither Ken nor Greta condemned me for missing the diagnosis. It was I who had been condemning myself through all my questions, nurturing my doubts about the past. Blinded perhaps by a mother's love, I had wanted the best for my daughter—and wanted, I'm sure, to believe that she was not struggling against any unusual handicap, but was simply a normal little girl. I could not redo the past, could only focus on trying to get the present right. Who knew what mistakes I might be making even now? Apparently, a life with guilt is always available to us.

Forgiveness of the past, hope for the future, work in the present… here was a motto to latch onto. As we pulled into the driveway, I welcomed the return home. I felt ready to accept what I still could not explain. I ruminated back over moments with my daughter:

"Mommy, can you help me read this big book before school tomorrow? Mom, do you think I have any chance of getting into a good college? Mother, can you see me getting into medical school?"

Yes. Absolutely. Yes, you can do it.

After looking directly into the sun on our walkway, I missed a step while entering the house. Ken and Greta, flanking me, caught me as I stumbled.

It felt as if we never missed a beat.

We were a family that had gone through many turbulent shoals together, and now we were navigating the revelation of Greta's dyslexia and attention deficit disorder. And, to look at us together on that sunny Sunday morning coming home from church, you would have to say we were doing just fine.

Recently, Greta received the results from her Internal Medicine Specialty Board Examination in the mail. She was so afraid to open the envelope that she just held it for awhile. Her husband was out of town, and she was alone in the house, so she took the letter into the kitchen and sat down on the floor. When she finally mustered the courage to open the envelope, she read: "Congratulations, the Board is pleased to notify you that you passed..." The pride on her face was evident even over the phone when she called to tell us, and that pride only increased with my husband and me.

* * *

Later, having come to terms with my debilitating guilt, I asked myself again how I could have missed this diagnosis of ADD. Then I remembered... *Physicians don't treat themselves or their family members. A lawyer who represents himself has a fool for a client.* Now I could add another maxim: educational diagnosticians and psychologists should recognize that trying to assess family members is hazardous. Personal involvement destroys the objectivity we require to make accurate assessments. Physician, heal someone other than thyself—or thy loved one!

chapter 10

the achievers

A ROLL CALL of celebrities, presidents, diplomats, generals, inventors, writers, and entrepreneurs who have struggled with learning disabilities would astonish you. If you, a member of your family, a neighbor, or a friend of yours has dyslexia or any other learning disability, you can certainly count yourself in distinguished company.

What is more, dyslexics and others with serious reading problems usually compensate for their disability by having one or more of the following strengths: better-than-average verbal skills, athletic prowess, outstanding ability in mathematics, exceptional creativity, and a knack for understanding other people's problems.

An uncanny ability to work around their weak spots enables dyslexics to survive as well as they do. Their ruses for keeping people from knowing of their reading or spelling problems are seemingly endless. Dave's taking a friend with him to New York to read a contract before he signed it, and Eric's choosing his words for a paper from among those he knew he could spell are just two examples of these survival skills.

Famous dyslexics, too, had to find ways to work around their language problems.

Thomas Edison's handwriting and spelling were atrocious; he dropped out of elementary school in the third grade. When Edison wrote to his mother as a grown man, his handwriting and spelling looked like a child's. I sometimes think fondly of Edison and his LD problems when I switch on a light.

Woodrow Wilson did not learn to read until he was about twelve years old. His mother and his sister finally brought his reading along, pumping him full of phonics. When he finally did master the skill of reading, he acquitted himself well, rising to become president first of Princeton University and then of the United States.

General George Patton, the great World War II hero, matriculated at West Point, but with scant ability to decipher words on a page! He paid other students to read his textbooks to him. Though he became a highly successful military commander, he never did learn to read very well. Some people have surmised that Patton's gruff ways with colleagues and others stemmed from his self-consciousness about his reading problems.

Winston Churchill once said that his mother read him through school, and after he married, his wife read him the rest of the way. He wrote his speeches and books largely by dictating to secretaries. Even as Prime Minister of Great Britain, he continued to struggle with difficulties in reading and writing.

Albert Einstein failed German all through school. One of his teachers wrote of him: "Albert is a lazy boy who never tries to do his work. He daydreams all the time." I wonder if Albert might have been dreaming about physics instead of language. His problems with language did not prevent him from becoming one of the most brilliant physicists and theoreticians in history.

New York Governor Nelson Rockefeller was tutored throughout his school years. As an adult he had his secretary write his speeches on a primary typewriter, dividing each word into syllables. In high school Rockefeller discovered his gift for public speaking and joined the debate team. He soon learned how to compensate for his deficiencies in written language by excelling in oral presentations.

Hans Christian Andersen had a terrible time with handwriting and spelling. He wrote and spelled so badly that his publisher couldn't read what he'd put down on paper. Fortunately, Andersen had a good friend who "translated" his scribblings so the publisher could read them.

Millions of us are glad he did as we enjoy "Thumbelina," "The Ugly Ducking," "The Princess and the Pea," "The Tinder Box," and scores of other enchanting tales. Hans Christian Andersen seemed to have everything against him: he was very poor, quite ugly and awkward, and he labored under a learning disability. He worked hard to overcome these obstacles, however, and never gave up—even when failure was staring him in the face. He continued to laugh and hope, though circumstances around him looked bleak.

We all know and continue to benefit from the contributions of these famous dyslexics: William Butler Yeats, F. Scott Fitzgerald, Auguste Rodin, Robert Lowell, William James, Demosthenes, Moses, Leonardo da Vinci, John Lennon, John F. Kennedy, Robert F. Kennedy, General William Westmoreland, Prince Charles, Dwight D. Eisenhower, Philip K. Wrigley, Governor Gaston Caperton, John F. Kennedy Jr., John Barnitt, Bruce Jenner, Earvin "Magic" Johnson, Greg Louganis, Daniel Stern, Tracey Gold, Cher, Tom Cruise, Harry Anderson, Henry Winkler, Anne Bancroft, and Jay Leno.

The contributions of famous—and not so famous—dyslexics to our society have clearly been substantial. Because of their learning problems, though, many dyslexics spend little time in the regular classroom. Or, when in the classroom, come to look upon it as a torture or prison sentence.

Often they are vilified or ridiculed by insensitive teachers and peers. Yet without proper attention, their tremendous potential for contributing to society can be lost or greatly diminished.

It's amazing how much we depend on the discoveries of people such as Thomas Edison, who dropped out of the third grade. George Patton and Albert Einstein both needed tutoring to make their way in school. These three men all achieved greatness, but the emotional trauma they endured because of their reading problems should not be a legacy for the generations of learning disabled that follow.

✿   ✿   ✿

Ignorance of learning disabilities still seems rampant among professional educators. Many children in today's schools are lost before they even really begin. Teachers unfamiliar with dyslexia or other learning disabilities fail to refer students for testing and remediation, while teachers who do have an understanding still haven't learned how to teach these students effectively. Too many school administrators also lack an adequate understanding of what's needed. They concern themselves with numbers of children on charts and numbers in budgets, rather than with measuring the effectiveness of academic programs (not only for dyslexics but for students in general).

A child who is dyslexic is often doomed to sub-par performance when he or she is limited to the basal reader provided for all children and the regular classroom teacher has no idea how to teach a child who learns differently. Often, students are all expected to follow the same reading path together. Those who can't make the climb are simply left to repeat the year, usually with the same ineffective teaching techniques in place.

Many school systems now group students with developmental disabilities (such as mental retardation, autism, and cerebral palsy), emotional disturbances, and learning disabilities together in classrooms. If there is a more harmful way to group exceptional children, I don't know what it is. The intelligence of people with learning disabilities is as good as, and can even be superior to, the intelligence of normally achieving students. We know this from current research, yet we continue to act counter to this knowledge by mixing students with learning disabilities in with children who are mentally retarded.

Children with learning disabilities are not mentally retarded. The potentials of the two groups are quite different. Furthermore, the students who are mentally retarded can become discouraged when they see their slower progress being compared with the progress of properly taught students with learning disabilities.

I'm even more concerned about the current trend for total inclusion. In this approach all exceptional children are integrated into the regular classroom and spend the whole day there. The idea is that a special education teacher will work with the regular classroom teacher to suggest appropriate materials and techniques for those with special needs. But how can one regular classroom teacher, even a "super-teacher" meet the needs of twenty normally-achieving children, one physically handicapped child, one mentally retarded child, two learning disabled children, and one child who has a visual problem? In my opinion, all the children will suffer.

My fear is that many of our children will be lost or fail to reach their potential if they spend too much time in the regular classroom and do not receive concentrated attention to their specific needs. Packing one classroom jam full of problems—an excess of problems—is not the way to solve any of those problems.

Every child needs to succeed in some way. If a child doesn't experience academic success, that child often becomes a bully, a goof-off, a drug abuser, or an emotional wreck. If we persist in forcing total inclusion in our schools, I believe we are going to produce more social and academic disasters than we've had up to now.

Each person in this book responded to dyslexia, and other learning disorders, in a different way. But they all have one thing in common—an absolute refusal to give up. Their lives also exemplify the pain and heartbreak that can result from problems affecting reading and written language, especially if those problems are misdiagnosed, ignored, or mistreated.

It is this pain and heartbreak of millions of the learning disabled in our society that resonates with me most in moments when I sit alone and think about where we are now in our understanding, and how much further we still have to go.

chapter 11

the future

WHAT IS THE present state of learning disabilities (LD) and what does the future hold? The future of learning disabilities is probably as uncertain as the definition of learning disabilities is controversial. It is sometimes troubling being a professional in a field plagued by significant disagreements. Discords are in evidence not only on the definitions but also on the best educational remediation for learning disabilities and the best way to structure learning disability programs. Let's look at some typically thorny questions and then consider possible resolutions.

Definition

A learning disability is the only debilitating condition that one can have in one county and not in another—in one state and not in another. What is the reason for this strange phenomenon? Is there a "regional cure"? No. It's just a matter of who is doing the defining. A precise and inclusive definition of dyslexia (and other learning disabilities) is urgently needed.[1]

The Specific Learning Disabilities Act of 1969 includes a definition of learning disabilities that has been very confusing for many professionals, parents, and others. It states that a person must have a severe discrepancy between ability and achievement in order to be diagnosed as having a learning disability. This definition has been included in Public Law 94-142 (now the Individuals with Disabilities Education Act [IDEA]), Section 504 of the

Rehabilitation Act, and the Americans with Disabilities Act (ADA) What federal legislation does not say is what is meant by a "severe discrepancy." Some school systems require one standard deviation between the standard scores of intellectual ability (IQ) and at least one achievement test score. Other school systems require one-and-one-half standard deviations, whereas others require two standard deviations. (One standard deviation is fifteen points when the mean is one hundred.) For example, if a student has an IQ of 115, he may be considered to have a learning disability in some geographical locations if the reading standard score is one hundred (one standard deviation discrepancy). In other locations, the definition may need to be as low as a standard score of eighty-five in order to meet the discrepancy requirement. My opinion is that we should place more emphasis on the specific problems each student is experiencing, rather than focusing so intently on test scores.

Also, there doesn't seem to be any provision for a mild case of LD: either the student must have a "severe discrepancy" or he or she doesn't have a problem that the school must address at all. Many of the more mildly disabled could benefit significantly from short-term educational remediation, after which they could probably be successful for the remainder of their school careers. As it is now, those who don't qualify to be diagnosed as having a severe discrepancy—and hence warrant the diagnosis of learning disabled—receive no help through the school system's Special Education program. In all probability, these may be the people who could benefit the most with the least monetary cost. If a minor problem isn't corrected in first, second, or third grade, it is possible that, without treatment, the minor problem could blossom into a catastrophe five or ten years later. It is much more cost effective to treat minor problems in the early years of school than major problems later on. We all know this—educational professionals and seasoned politicians especially. We simply must quit paying lip service to this truism and begin to take appropriate early intervention action immediately.

The Price of Illiteracy

Three-quarters of the country's jobless are illiterate; those who do find jobs can expect to earn only fifty-eight percent of what literate employees make. Currently, seventy percent of a cross section of jobs around the country require a reading level of ninth grade or higher. If the educational system in this country continues to graduate 2.5 million functionally illiterate students into the work force annually, unemployment and its attendant ills will only worsen. As illiteracy increases, America's rank as an industrial power will slide. Illiteracy threatens the very fabric of American political and social life, because democracy relies on educated voters.[2] As we have learned many times in history, an illiterate population cannot make choices that are well-informed or well-reasoned.

A 1989 report from IBM states, "Society must re-prioritize what is important and what is not important ... knowledge level and the competence of our people is the single most important asset we have. We cannot continue to be competitive if one out of three of our kids fails to learn the basic skills."[3] The importance of this statement becomes clear when one realizes that the number of unskilled and semi-skilled jobs in the United States is rapidly declining.

Today the majority of school systems in America does not actively teach reading to students beyond the fifth or sixth grades. Many students enroll in H.E.L.P. at Marshall University, where I teach, as college freshmen who are functional illiterates. And most of them tell us that they have had no instruction in basic reading skills for the last seven years or more.

The Teaching of Reading

Problems involved in the ways in which we teach reading have been mentioned previously; however, it seems advisable to briefly discuss the problem as I see it. When a school has one reading series for every child, how can we expect every child to respond positively?

In the future I hope that schools will have several possibilities available and that some attempt will be made to discover how each child learns best. Countless research articles have reported that phonics seems to be the method that reaches the greatest number of people. There is a growing interest in a multi-sensory approach to learning, and this seems to be able to reach some children and adults when other attempts have failed.

Until our schools accept that people learn in different ways and must be taught accordingly, we will continue to have large numbers of students joining the ranks of the illiterate as adults.

The Increase of ADHD

In 1937 hyperactivity and distractibility were cited for the first time in professional literature. The first professional recognition of this disorder was accorded in 1968 in the second edition of the *Diagnostic and Statistical Manual of Mental Disorders* (DSM-2) when the term "attention deficit disorder" was introduced. Today the number of ADD cases has grown significantly. Dr. Larry Silver, an author and expert in the field of ADD at Georgetown University School of Medicine, writes that when parents complete a rating scale, as much as thirty percent of the school age population may have attention deficit hyperactivity disorder (ADHD) to varying degrees. When teachers complete the same scale, the numbers range from ten to twenty percent.[4] The most recent numbers show estimates that thirty to seventy percent of children who have learning disabilities will also have ongoing symptoms of ADHD as they enter adulthood.[5]

There are other estimates from professionals, but we do not know exactly how many people actually have ADHD. One thing is certain: the number grows daily. This may be the result of over-diagnosis; on the other hand, the increase is more likely the result of a greater recognition and awareness of this problem.

When reading a newspaper, magazine, or watching television,

one soon becomes aware how frequently ADHD is the topic. More often than not, the coverage lacks objectivity. We read stories about elementary schools that almost force parents into having their children medicated with Ritalin. We see parents and teachers on TV who tell of children waiting in long lines to get their Ritalin. There is almost always an air of hostility in the reports.

In my experience, when a child is treated by a knowledgeable physician who has experience in the treatment of ADHD, this biased scenario does not exist. Certainly, there are some children who are incorrectly diagnosed and others who are incorrectly medicated, but isn't this true in everything? As we learn more about ADHD, its symptoms, and treatments, the numbers of children who are diagnosed and medicated properly increases.

One of my concerns about ADHD involves Supplemental Security Income (SSI) and the increasing numbers of children who are receiving monthly benefits because they have ADHD. It is wise to provide funds for severely handicapped children who have expensive medical bills, but the child who has been diagnosed as having ADHD can usually be medicated for less than fifty dollars per month. It does not require other support of the child or the family. In my opinion, ADHD does not require federal assistance; it is my hope that current large federal outlays will be curtailed and the funds devoted to problems of greater need in education of disabled children and adolescents.

Sometimes when we suspect that a child has ADHD and ask the parents to fill out a checklist of possible indicators, they will respond "no" to the majority of questions. We usually give the parents some material about ADHD to read and have them come back at a later date, hoping that time and the reading material will jog their memories. Usually, one or both parents will say something like, "Last week, when you asked us about ADHD, we didn't think that Jimmy had any of the symptoms. We talked about it a lot, and now we think that maybe we weren't being truly honest with ourselves. We had also forgotten that my brother can't sit still for more than a few minutes and that he is always in trouble because he is so impulsive. Our son finds it nearly impossible to be still for more than ten minutes. There are other things, too... Could we go through those checklists again?" The responses often differ significantly the second time around.

Of course, there are children and adults who consistently deny the presence of any of the symptoms of ADHD. Recently, when I spoke to a H.E.L.P. student who is now a junior, he told me that he had always denied that he had ADHD symptoms because, "I can't hide the fact that I have LD. You can see it in my spelling and hear it in my reading, but I can hide ADHD from you pretty well. I'm about as different as I'm willing to be. I don't want any more problems." I asked him if hiding his problem made it easier to live with. He smiled sheepishly and said, "You may wear me down soon. Don't give up on me, Dr. G." I won't, and when he fails his next test because of his difficulties in focusing and organizing, perhaps I can convince him to get medical help.

Sometimes a college student becomes more accepting of ADHD when I say, "If you had diabetes, would you take insulin every day?" The response, of course, is "yes." I continue, "Then when you have a neurologically-based problem like ADHD, what's wrong with taking the correct medication that is prescribed by a physician who is experienced in this area of medicine?"

Alternative methods of treating ADHD seem to be increasing. Health food stores and mail order houses seem to profit significantly from parents' quests to find ways to help their children learn to focus, concentrate, and improve memory and organizational skills. Although a limited body of research has, as of this writing, indicated that alternative approaches are not successful, many parents continue to look for solutions here. It will be enlightening to see if any of these treatments provide beneficial results that withstand scientific scrutiny, allowing LD/ADHD children, adolescents, and adults to focus on one thing at a time, to become more organized, and less impulsive.

A college student gave me the best definition of ADHD that I have ever heard. Dave, a sophomore in college who had been battling with his ADHD problems on a daily basis, strode into my office one day with a look on his face that told me he had something important to say. I looked at him expectantly. "I just figured out what ADHD is, Dr. G," this sophomore began.

"Oh, and what is it, Dave?" I asked.

"You know when you get in your car, you turn your car radio on?" he asked. I nodded affirmatively. "Then you hit the scan button to get a sampling of what the choices are at that time. You find a station you want to listen to, so you hit the scan button again, except it won't stop scanning, no matter how hard you hit the button. ADHD is like that. You are listening to a lecture, and you want to just listen to that lecture. You know that your mid-term exam will depend on your getting down what you are hearing. But then all of these other thoughts start bombarding your mind. You want to stop 'going around the dial,' but you can't stop. You just go 'round and 'round."

Inclusion

One of the greatest concerns that I have about education today is inclusion. Let me explain what I believe inclusion is. Partial inclusion means that a student will spend part of the school day in the regular classroom and part of the day in the special education (learning disabilities) classroom. The time spent in each environment will be determined by the school placement committee, which includes the child's parents, the special education teacher, a representative of the superintendent of schools, the principal, the school psychologist, sometimes the student, and any others deemed appropriate.

Total inclusion means that the student receives all services in the regular classroom. In the event that a tenth grader requires reading and spelling remediation because of dyslexia, for example, that must be done in the regular classroom.[6] A special education teacher may provide the service or the regular classroom teacher may be given special materials to use with the student, along with directions.[7] If I were a tenth grade student, I would refuse to participate in remedial reading if it had to be done in the presence of my unaffected peers. I would be terribly embarrassed that my reading skills were poor and would do whatever I had to, to keep my friends from knowing anything about my reading problem. When you are in a classroom, you can hear almost everything that goes on in that room. Special reading and spelling instruction does not go unnoticed by the bullies, the burnouts, and other maladjusted peers. The teasing and chastising that occur are thoroughly humiliating, especially to a person who is sensitive and easily hurt. Bullies seem to have a sixth sense that enables them to pick up on others' weak spots, and they quickly zoom in to create a fracas. Typically, they hope to make themselves look better than the victims of their harassment. Research has been very clear. A student with a language-based learning disability (LLD) has more than twice the chance of having a psychiatric disorder as one who does not have an LLD.[8]

In an ideal society I believe that total inclusion can work, but we have nothing approaching that at this time. The discipline problems in our schools are a serious problem, and no one seems to know exactly what should be done to alleviate this problem. One thing that will definitely not improve discipline in America's classrooms is to put children with the range of disabling conditions in the regular classroom with the "normal" students and their problems. Most regular classroom teachers flirt with early burnout as it is. I fear that if we further complicate matters, the result will be unbearable for America's teachers. It should be noted that few of our classroom teachers have been trained to deal with children and adolescents who have learning disabilities. Simple tips, such as placing a child with reading problems near a good student who will be that student's "buddy," can make a significant difference in the success level of a disabled student. The teacher needs to clarify the rules, such as those relating to the buddy system. The buddy may explain any directions that aren't understood, may spell words that the student doesn't know how to spell, and may copy assignments from the board, etc.[9] Another tactic that helps is seating a student who has ADHD near the front of the room so that there will be fewer distractions between the student and the teacher. If the teacher's desk is a busy place, a seat too near the desk would not be wise. Simple modifications such as these can mean the difference between failure for a student, a headache for the teacher, or a very satisfactory day of school for both of them.

I have graduate students from several states who tell me that they have or have had students commingled in their "regular" classrooms with IQs that may be as low as thirty-five and as high as 145. That range of intelligence would already be difficult to deal with, but add to that students whose physical needs are quite demanding—such as those who are not toilet-trained or who drool constantly—and you have a job that may quickly overtax the average teacher. This morning I talked with a graduate student who could be an excellent teacher, but he feels he is in a hopeless situation. He teaches six periods a day, and in each class he has some children who have learning disabilities, some who have behavioral disorders, and some who are mentally retarded. He has as many as twenty students at a time. He sadly stated that he thought he could teach the LD students something, but he was so busy breaking up fights and enforcing acceptable behavior that he couldn't teach anyone much of anything.

If inclusion is funded properly, it has a much better chance of succeeding. But how many school systems see inclusion simply as a means of slashing expenses? I am afraid that many are trying to cut corners in ways that will antagonize as few people as possible, and cutting special education programs seems to be one of their favorite approaches.

Juvenile Delinquency

If we continue to fail to teach our students with learning disabilities how to read, we will soon have to enlarge our facilities for juvenile delinquents. There seems to be a direct relationship between failure to read and juvenile delinquency. I learned this first hand when I taught delinquent boys early in my career. As they learned to read they acted out their hostilities less and less. One fourteen-year-old said to me, "Nah, Ms. Guyer, I ain't robbin' no more cars. I ain't robbin' no more nothin'. You know why? I'm editor of the school newspaper now. That's a lot better'n robbin' cars and gettin' picked up by the police." This boy was enrolled in a Learning Disabilities Center full-time for three years as he learned to read. He had daily instruction in reading and spelling for two hours and weekly group and individual counseling. Yes, this was expensive—but it was much less expensive than the exorbitant cost of housing him in a juvenile detention center and later in a prison. And that's where I firmly believe this young man would be today if he hadn't learned to read and thereby raised his self-esteem. I might also add that he would not have been editor of the school newspaper in a regular school, but in the LD Center he was able to develop his good leadership potential. Today this individual is married and has three children. He works as a supervisor in a factory. Instead of being a drain on society, he is a positive influence. He also has a life that is worthwhile. Isolating students certainly has its drawbacks; but there are definitely advantages to separating students with serious behavior and learning problems from their peers until you can reach them and prepare them to return to the regular classroom. If the man I cited here did not learn to read, and if he eventually went to prison, he would be a financial drain on the state and the quality of his life would be marginal.

I saw this sort of rise in self-esteem and in personal productivity happen over and over with pre-delinquent and delinquent boys and girls when they were able to benefit from suitable programs.

For some reason I have never completely understood, students equate being able to read with being a "good" or "worthwhile" person. Many teenagers have said to me, "No, Ms. Guyer, there's no way I can read. I'm just no good. I'm not worth nobody spending no money on me." It is sad to see people give up at age thirteen or fourteen. They have given up any thoughts of "the good life" and are ready to settle for any quick fix that comes their way, be it drugs, crime, sex, or whatever.

Learning Styles

Probably the thing that keeps me awake at night the most is the conviction that deep down inside each of those teenagers is a beautiful person begging to be released. Somehow we must find the funds necessary to teach these special people to read before we lose them. When we expose all of the children in a classroom to one basal reading series, we condemn a percentage of those students to failure before they begin. Each person has a learning style that is unique. Why don't we do some limited screening to determine how each student learns best and then expose each child to a reading program that espouses that approach? Doesn't that make more sense than trying to teach everyone in the same way and condemning both them and us to a high failure rate? Some students may need to see and hear something in order to learn; others may need to see and write or trace with the index finger; others may need to hear, see, and write or trace in order to learn best. If we could have three reading programs and assign children to the appropriate ones, this could make quite a difference in the number of children who learn to read successfully.[10] And the end result would be more students who were successful in school. I firmly believe that we would have a significant decrease in the number of juvenile delinquents that we are producing in America today.

A suggestion that may help to improve our success rate in teaching reading is to have spelling, reading, written language, and handwriting all taught as a part of the same curriculum. For example, the new words we have for reading would also be our spelling words; they would also be the words we include in our writing experiences as much as possible. Handwriting classes would focus on the letters and words that are in the reading and spelling sections. In this manner, students have more opportunities to build a bridge to what they are learning. This also makes it easier to process the information through all of the sensory channels. In this way more students may experience success. Granted, textbook publishers who relish producing separate volumes for each activity (i.e., spelling books, readers, and composition guides), may not find this approach to their liking. But I am convinced by personal experience that combining these approaches works (and can save money).

Computer-Based Learning

Of all the inventions and materials that are becoming increasingly available to students, the one that holds the most promise to the LD/ADHD students is computer-based learning. Computer-based learning (CBL) holds great promise for the LD student in the following ways:

- ► CBL increases the retention rate;
- ► CBL can be used for adolescents or adults functioning on any level;
- ► CBL promotes greater learning effectiveness and faster progress;
- ► CBL can provide unlimited repetition for rote memorization and causes no embarassment for the student who needs repetition;
- ► CBL makes it possible to carefully structure learning;
- ► CBL provides a motivating factor for those having difficulty participating in a literacy program due to personal, economic, geographic, or other factors.[11]

When multimedia is involved, it can bring to life the total learning experience. Multimedia incorporates text, graphics, audio, digitized speech, photographs, animation, full-motion video, and interactive designs. Multimedia presents ideas in ways that draw students and users into the excitement of learning. Using multimedia programs also helps students take advantage of their natural curiosity by allowing them to interact with the medium to acquire new information.

Virtual reality attempts to involve the heretofore reluctant student in an exciting learning experience. A person enters this synthetic world through a head mount with stereoscopic goggles and a data glove, which are used to change images and options presented by the program. Some experts in the field predict that soon it will be possible to transfer everything we do to educate students using words and pictures into a virtual experience. The location, scale, density of information, interactivity, responsiveness, time, and degrees of participation can all be varied with the variety of technologies currently available.[12] The additional stimulation, colors, and sound will make it easier for the student with ADHD to focus on the task at hand. The student can also progress through a program at the rate that is ideal for him or her. Any failure a student may experience can be kept secret from others nearby. Total immersion in CBL provides many more learning possibilities for students who have difficulty learning. I can remember reading several years ago that we recall twenty-five percent of what we hear, forty-five percent of what we see and hear, and eighty percent or more of what we experience. It is time that we allow our students more extended opportunities to become actively involved in learning, and then we will see a much higher rate of success.

The Gifted Students

Finally, we must begin to recognize and diagnose the learning problems of gifted students at an early age. Today, many gifted LD/ADHD students survive until post-secondary school at varying levels. Some are able to survive in very competitive and challenging environments such as law or medical school. When finally diagnosed, they vividly describe how they have always known that they were different, how they have always worked much harder and longer than their peers, and how their self-esteem has suffered because they have never been able to function up to their potential levels.[13]

Innumerable educational problems now confront America's children with learning disabilities. There are, however, many assets. I have attempted to list both problems and resources. One often forgotten asset involves the creativity and empathy found in most students who have learning disabilities. Characteristically, many LD students have "people skills" that many others do not possess; and their caring nature makes them ideally suited to work in human service. Learning disabled medical students, with whom we have worked in H.E.L.P., struggle to survive during the basic science years of medical school. Then, when they move through the third and fourth years, centered more on practical exercises, they usually excel. Reading is more focused on one topic; less reading is required; and the students have an opportunity to get "hands on" experiences about what they are reading. The students who have excellent verbal and social skills usually shine during the clinical years of medical school, whereas the A students from the first few years sometimes do not fare as well because they don't have the outstanding interpersonal skills that the upper years require. This is a prime example of how we learn in different ways and how we demonstrate our knowledge differently.

The problems that are present in the field of learning disabilities today are not difficult to locate. The future promises to be a challenge as well. Sometimes being a teacher can be disappointing and frustrating; however, I have always been an optimist. Dr. Norman Vincent Peale convinced me many years ago that you are much better off when you engage in positive thinking. Thoughts are powerful things. On occasions when I became so discouraged that I could hardly bear to continue teaching, I have usually had sudden, phenomenal success with someone who helped me to see that what I was doing was on target or otherwise worthwhile.

In the classic Jimmy Stewart film, *It's a Wonderful Life*, Stewart's character, George Bailey, becomes so discouraged that he wishes he'd never been born. He gets his wish — and the opportunity to see what life for others would be like if he hadn't been there. He is shocked to see the difference he has made in people's lives. Being a teacher is like that. And being a teacher involved with students who have learning disabilities is a double, or triple dose. There is nothing to compare to seeing the sparkle return to the eyes of a child who was once without hope, to crying with an adult when he joyously reads his first short book at age forty-two, or to knowing that a student of yours took his girlfriend out to dinner and read the menu all by himself for the first time — and knew how to hold it right side up. Being a teacher affords a priceless opportunity to change lives for the better. I am proud of my peers, and glad to be able to count myself among their number.

✝   ✝   ✝

chapter 12

epilogue

TWENTY YEARS AGO, when I began speaking in public about people with learning disabilities and dyslexia, it occurred to me that it was easier to share what could be dull and boring facts if they were presented in the form of a story. So I began telling anecdotes about previous and current students, and I saw immediately that audiences seldom moved or coughed when I told a story. Many participants of conferences, members of PTAs and other organizations have made a point of telling me how interesting my presentations are. Many have said, "I can't tell you how much better I understand my child now that I've heard you speak." It is my conviction that understanding was enhanced by the anecdotal information I shared, and that those who were in the audience had been much more attentive than they would have been if my talk had been more like a textbook. It is not unusual to see several people wipe their eyes while I am telling a story—a story with a purpose.

It is my goal to give people hope through the stories that I share with you. Perhaps a parent, teacher, or the person involved will begin to see that the situation is not hopeless. If a depressed and dejected parent reads about Andy, perhaps that teacher or parent will find the courage to refuse to give up "the good fight."

Inclusion is on the lips of most of us who are involved in education. Regular classroom teachers, administrators, psychologists, and parents must learn more about the symptoms of learning disabilities. Perhaps reading about Dave, the genius who was an inmate in federal prison, will enable the regular classroom teacher to see the necessity for diagnosing a child's learning problems as early as possible. Often the symptoms of learning disabilities are overlooked in very bright children because their intelligence allows them to cope so well. As our society becomes more cognizant of the symptoms of dyslexia and other learning disabilities, as well as attention deficit disorder, we should be able to diagnose the causes of academic problems at an earlier age, thereby eliminating or decreasing the "scar tissue" that develops during times of failure. Perhaps *The Pretenders* is one means of doing this.

—Barbara Guyer

Oh yes, I'm the Great Pretender,
Pretending I'm doing well.
My need is such,
I pretend too much,
I'm lonely but no one can tell.
Oh yes, I'm the Great Pretender…

— Buck Ram
"The Great Pretender"

Notes

for Chapter 11

1 G. R. Lyon, "Toward a definition of dyslexia" *Annals of Dyslexia* 1995, 45: 3-30.

2 A. Barber, "Meeting the literacy challenge: Creating a nation of learners" *Electronic Learning* July 20, 1989, 3275: 68-70.

3 James Dezell, "Investing in America's future: Interview with Jim Dezell" *Electronic Learning* 1989, 8: 4, 9-12.

4 Larry B. Silver, *Attention-Deficit Hyperactivity Disorder: A Clinical Guide to Diagnosis and Treatment* (Washington, D.C.: American Psychiatric Press Inc., 1992).

5 R. Barkley, C. Edelbrook, M. Fischer, & Smallish; L. Bellack & R. Black (in press). "The adolescent outcome of hyperactive children diagnosed by research criteria: 1. An eight year prospective follow-up study" *Journal of the American Academy of Child and Adolescent Psychiatry*. In N. Gregg, C. Hoy & A. Gay (Eds.), *Adults with Learning Disabilities: Theoretical and Practical Perspectives* (New York: The Guilford Press, 1996).

6 W. Bender, *Learning Disabilities: Characteristics, Identification, and Teaching Strategies*, 2nd Ed. (Boston: Allyn & Bacon, 1995).

7 M. Friend & L. Cook (Instructors), "The New Mainstreaming," (March 1992).

8 Joseph Beitchman & Jane Hood, "Psychiatric risk for children with speech and language disorders" *Journal of Abnormal Child Psychology* June 1990, vol. 18, no. 3: 283-296.

9 Suzanne Stevens, *The Learning Disabled Child: Ways That Parents Can Help*. (Winston-Salem, North Carolina: John F. Blair, 1980).

10 S. Banks, B. Guyer, & K. Guyer, "Spelling improvement for college students who are dyslexic." *Annals of Dyslexia* 1993, 43: 186-93.

11 P. Fahey, "Adult literacy learning and computer technology: Features of effective computer-assisted learning systems." ED338867, Paper presented at the Alberta Association for Adult Literacy, Alberta, Canada, November 22, 1991: 27.

12 Hillary McLellan, "Virtual Reality: Visualization in three dimensions—in art, science & visual literacy" *Selected Readings from the Annual Conference of the International Visual Literacy Association, Pittsburgh, September 30-October 4, 1992* (1993).

13 B. Guyer, "Dyslexic doctors: A resource in need of discovery" *Southern Medical Journal* 1988, 81: 1151-54.

Glossary

attention deficit disorder (ADD) and *attention deficit hyperactivity disorder* (ADHD) persons with ADHD demonstrate a persistent pattern of inattention and/or hyperactivity-impulsivity that is more frequent and severe than in individuals at a comparable level of development. Symptoms include: short attention span, distractibility, hyperactivity, and impulsivity. People with ADHD tend to have a higher prevalence of learning disabilities like dyslexia. Can often be corrected with medications such as Ritalin.

Education professionals are still debating whether other forms of non-pharmaceutical treatments, such as anti-oxidant supplements, dietary changes, exercise, and behavior management, have any effect in alleviating ADHD. So far, research does not support these methods.

autism a developmental disability; impaired or abnormal development with regard to communication and social interaction, as well as a limited repertoire of interests and activity. About three-quarters of people with autism are also diagnosed with mental retardation. Manifestations of the disorder vary greatly, however, as does the intelligence level of persons with autism. Many autistics seem to "live in a world of their own," with little regard for the people around them.

college students with LD this is a fairly new area of Special Education. Research is beginning to indicate that certain LD students can and should complete college.

developmental disability a disorder that impairs a person's physical or cognitive development. Includes cerebral palsy, mental retardation, epilepsy, autism, and Down syndrome.

discrepancy the belief that children and adults with LD have abnormal growth development which results in significant differences in standardized measures of intelligence and certain areas of academic skills.

distractibility a tendency to be drawn away from a task to other stimuli in the environment.

dyslexia a term that indicates a difficulty with language, either spoken or written. In early years one may exhibit reversals and transpositions (e.g., *b/d, form/from*).

hyperactivity a much higher level of activity that is usually present by age seven. In-class behavior usually includes excessive fidgeting and/or inappropriate movement in the classroom.

impulsivity a tendency to act first and think later. Richard Lavoie describes this in a colorful way as, "Ready! Fire! Aim!"

inclusion a philosophy that endorses placing students with disabilities in the regular classroom. The Special Education teacher may provide services to the student through direct teaching, as a consultant, or monitoring the LD student as carefully as possible.

Individuals with Disabilities Education Act (IDEA) originally Public Law 94-142, this legislation gives every handicapped student the right to be educated in a manner that is as good as what is provided for normal children. The handicapped children are also to be educated in what experts feel is "the least restrictive environment". That phrase has created much dissension among professionals and parents. It is still being argued.

learning by association one learns by associating what is already known with what needs to be learned. Information, to be meaningful, does not exist on an island. There must be "bridges" to connect it to the "mainland" of one's knowledge.

learning disability (LD) a person with nominal or above average intelligence who learns differently from others. This learning difference exists throughout one's lifetime, and a person must personally discover how learning occurs best and most efficiently. If not treated, LD may seriously affect the quality of one's life.

mental retardation a developmental disability; significantly subaverage intellectual functioning which affects a person's ability to adapt and learn. Mental retardation is indicated by a level of intelligence of 70 or below as measured by an IQ test. Mental retardation is not a learning disability and is distinct from disorders such as dyslexia and attention deficit disorder.

Montessori School named after Maria Montessori, M.D., who developed a multi-sensory educational program for mentally retarded children in Italy and who later found that this program also worked quite well with children of normal intelligence. This innovative program spread to the United States, and today we have Montessori schools across our country. Children learn everything concretely before they are exposed to the information in an abstract manner. There is no competition between students until they are old enough to be secure in what they are doing.

multisensory learning instructional techniques that employ the use of more than one sensory channel at a time.

Orton-Gillingham approach developed by neurologist, Dr. Samuel Orton, and psychologist, Anna Gillingham in the late 1920s. Still used today (or one of its many adaptations), this is a multi-sensory, phonetic program that teaches reading, spelling, written language, and handwriting. The program is especially recommended for dyslexics, but seems to work with many others who have had difficulty learning to read and write.

Public Law 94-142 see *Individuals with Disabilities Education Act (IDEA).*

Rehabilitation Act, section 504 guarantees a number of rights to the post-secondary student with a learning disability, including testing accommodations, course substitutions, and extension of time to complete degree.

resource room a room where an LD student (and others) may go for part of the school day to receive specific assistance from a teacher who has been specially trained to work with the student's problems.

self-concept the opinion that a person has of his or her worth.

self-contained class students remain in one or more separate classes for the entire day. They are not in the regular classroom, unless they may be assigned to have music, art, or physical education with their peers.

sight-word approach an approach to reading in which students are taught to recognize whole words in context and do not learn letter sounds.

Simultaneous Oral Spelling (S.O.S.) part of the Orton-Gillingham approach. The teacher decreases the complexity of what is required of students when they write.

Wechsler Intelligence Scale for Children-III (WISC-III) and **Wechsler Adult Intelligence Scale-Revised (WAIS-R)** are considered by most professionals to be the best and most popular intelligence tests for use in evaluating intelligence when learning problems seem to be present.

Woodcock-Johnson Tests of Achievement is a highly respected, lengthy evaluation of achievement in children and adults. The test must be administered by a trained professional to one student at a time.

Readings

Amen, D. *Don't Shoot Yourself in the Foot: A Program to End Self-Defeating Behavior Forever.* New York: Warner Books. 1992.

Banks, S., B. Guyer and K. Guyer. "A study of medical students and physicians referred for learning disabilities." *Annals of Dyslexia* 1995. 45: 233-245.

Cohen, N., M. Davine, N. Horodezky, L. Lipsett, and L. Isaacson. "Unsuspected language impairment in psychiatrically disturbed children: Prevalence and language and behavioral characteristics." *Journal of American Academy of Child and Adolescent Psychiatry* 1993. 32(3): 595-603.

Esser, G., M. Schmidt, and L. Rosenberg. "Epidemiology and course of psychiatric disorders in school-age children." *Journal of Child Psychiatry and Psychology* 1990. 31(2): 243-63.

Ferrett, S. *Peak Performance.* Burr Ridge, Illinois: Irwin Mirrow Press. 1994.

Gerber, Paul & Henry Rieff. *Learning Disabilities in Adulthood: Persisting Problems and Evolving Issues.* Boston: Andover Medical Publishers. 1994.

Hallowell, E. & J. Ratey. *Driven to Distraction: Recognizing and Coping with Attention Deficit Disorder from Childhood through Adulthood.* New York: Pantheon Books. 1994.

Levine, M. *Keeping Ahead in School*. Cambridge: Educators Publishing Service Inc. 1990.

MacCracken, Mary. *Turnabout Children*. Boston, Massachusetts: Little, Brown and Co. 1986.

Rief, S. *How to Reach and Teach* ADD/ADHD *Children*. West Nyack, New York: The Center for Applied Research in Education. 1993.

Silver, Larry B. *Attention-Deficit Hyperactivity Disorder: A Clinical Guide to Diagnosis and Treatment* Washington, D.C.: American Psychiatric Press Inc., 1992.

Stevens, S. *The Learning Disabled Child: Ways that Parents Can Help*. Winston-Salem, North Carolina: John F. Blair Publishers. 1996.

Stoner, J., M. Farrell & B. Guyer. *College: How Students with Dyslexia Can Maximize the Experience*. Baltimore: The Orton Dyslexia Society.

Vail, Priscilla. *Learning Styles: Food for Thought and 130 Practical Tips for Teachers* K-4. Rosemont, New Jersey: Modern Learning Press. 1996.

Resources

Association on Higher Education (AHEAD)
P.O. BOX 21192, Columbus, Ohio 43221
(614) 488-4972 FAX (614) 488-1174
AHEAD *is a multi-cultural, international organization of professionals who attempt to help people with disabilities who attend college. The group offers training programs, workshops, publications, and an annual conference. AHEAD is growing, and it is meeting a definite need at the college level.*

The Attention Deficit Information Network, Inc. (AD-IN)
475 Hillside Avenue, Needham, Massachusetts 02194 (617) 455-9895
AD-IN *offers support and information to families of children and adults with* ADD, *as well as to the professionals who work with them.* AD-IN *has 60 parent and adult chapters. Has information packets for children and adults with* ADD.

Children and Adults with Attention Deficit Disorder (CHADD)
499 Northwest 70th Avenue, Suite 308, Plantation, Florida 33317
(305) 587-3700 FAX (305) 587-4599
CHADD *is a parent-based organization that dispenses information on* ADD *and coordinates more than 460 parent support groups. Their semi-annual magazine,* CHADDER, *and newsletter,* Chadderbox, *make worthwhile contributions to the field.*

Council for Learning Disabilities (CLD)
P.O. BOX 40303, Overland Park, Kansas 66204
(913) 492-8755 FAX (913) 492-2546
CLD *is a professional organization designed to improve the education and lives of those with learning disabilities.*

HEALTH RESOURCE CENTER
One Dupont Circle, Suite 800, Washington, D.C. 20036
TOLL-FREE (800) 544-3284 FAX (202) 833-4760
The HEALTH RESOURCE CENTER *is a national clearinghouse on post-sec-*
ondary education for adults with disabilities as a program of the American
Council on Education. Response to inquiries and many free, excellent pub-
lications combine to make this a very helpful and worthwhile center.

LEARNING DISABILITIES ASSOCIATION OF AMERICA (LDA)
4156 Library Road, Pittsburgh, Pennsylvania 15234
(412) 341-1515 FAX (412) 344-0224
LDA *is an advocacy organization that provides information and referral ser-*
vices. The 50,000 members have chapters in most states. LDA *prints*
Newsbriefs, *an excellent bi-monthly newsletter for parents, professionals,*
and adults with LD.

NATIONAL ADULT LITERACY AND LEARNING DISABILITIES CENTER
(NATIONAL ALLD CENTER)
Academy for Educational Development
1875 Connecticut Avenue, NW, Washington, D.C. 20009-1202
(202) 884-8185 TOLL-FREE (800) 953-ALLD
Funded by the National Institute for Literacy, NATIONAL ALLD CENTER *is*
a national resource for information on learning disabilities and their
impact on the provision of literacy services. They attempt to assist teachers
to teach adults with learning disabilities more successfully.

NATIONAL NETWORK OF LEARNING DISABLED ADULTS (NNLDA)
808 North 82nd Street, Suite F2, Scottsdale, Arizona 85257
(602) 941-5112.
NNLDA *provides information and referral services for learning disabled*
adults who want to join a support group or need networking opportunities.
A quarterly newsletter is published.

ORTON DYSLEXIA SOCIETY
8600 LaSalle Road, Suite 382, Baltimore, Maryland 21286-2044
(410) 296-0232 TOLL-FREE (800) 222-3123 FAX (410) 321-5069
This is an international scientific and educational organization that is concerned with dyslexia (specific language disability). Local and state branches serve as resources for all who have an interest in this population. A quarterly newsletter, Perspectives, *and a journal,* Annals of Dyslexia, *are well written.*

REBUS INSTITUTE
1499 Bayshore Boulevard, Suite 146, Burlingame, California 94010
(415) 697-7424 FAX (415) 697-3734
This is a national organization dedicated to the study and dissemination of information on adult issues related to LD *and* ADD.

RECORDINGS FOR THE BLIND AND DYSLEXIC (RFB)
20 Roszel Road, Princeton, New Jersey 20542
(609) 452-0606 TOLL-FREE (800) 221-4792
RFB *is a not-for-profit organization that provides educational books on tape that are lent free of charge (except for a modest one-time payment). Books on computer disk are beginning to be available and will increase in time.*

About the Author

BARBARA PRIDDY GUYER grew up in Richmond, Virginia, where she attended the public schools. Her experiences at Virginia Commonwealth University instilled in her a great love of teaching that she has never lost. She has received additional degrees from The Ohio State University, the University of Virginia, and West Virginia University College of Graduate Studies.

Dr. Guyer and her husband Dr. Kenneth Guyer have lived in five states, which has broadened her teaching experiences. During her career, she has taught grades two through six, remedial reading, learning disability classes, and reading to inmates in a women's prison in Virginia. She has also been a supervisor of special education, a principal of two learning disability centers, and has coordinated the learning disabilities graduate program at Marshall University since 1975. She began the H.E.L.P. Program (Higher Education for Learning Problems) in 1981 as a support for undergraduate students with dyslexia, attention deficit disorder, and other learning disabilities. She also started the Medical H.E.L.P. Program in 1986 for medical students and physicians needing remedial reading support; to date, more than two hundred medical students have successfully completed this program.

Dr. Guyer and her husband have two daughters, Greta and Jennifer. Through them, she has gained an understanding of learning problems, dyslexia, and attention deficit disorder from a parent's perspective. The compassion she feels for students, parents, and teachers comes through in her writing and is exemplified in her many accomplishments.

A Note on the Type

The text of this book was set in Electra, a typeface designed in 1935 by the renowned designer and illustrator William A. Dwiggins (1880-1956). A standard book typeface since its release due to the evenness of design and high legibility, this face cannot be classified as either modern or old style. It is not based on any historical model, nor does it echo any particular period or style. It avoids the extreme contrasts between thick and thin elements that mark most modern faces, and it gives a feeling of fluidity, warmth, personality, and speed.

Printed and bound by BookCrafters,
Chelsea, Michigan

Illustrations by John Cartwright and Cliff Elliott,
who have both overcome learning difficulties

Designed by Alex Lubertozzi